Treasure for

the Heart

Treasure for the Heart

By

Reba Jean Smith

Word of His Mouth Publishers
Mooresboro, NC

All Scripture quotations are taken from the **King James Version** of the Bible.

ISBN: 978-1-941039-49-6
Printed in the United States of America
82024 Reba Jean Smith

Word of His Mouth Publishers
Mooresboro, NC
www.wordofhismouth.com

Table of Contents

Hidden Treasure

Everyone loves a good treasure hunt; even as adults, we enjoy the occasional scavenger hunt, always looking for the prize. Our hearts should always be searching for that incorruptible treasure that money cannot buy. Hebrews 11:6 reminds us, *"But without faith it is impossible to please him: for he that cometh to God must believe that he is, and that he is a rewarder of them that diligently seek him."* When we believe in Jesus Christ for our salvation, we must then continue to believe in Him for our everyday living. When we trust in Him, He rewards us!

How do we find this hidden treasure, this reward for our faith? Matthew 13:44-52 shares a parable of Jesus that speaks concerning this treasure hunt. Let's look at verses forty-four through forty-six as we, too, search for this hidden treasure for the heart.

"Again, the kingdom of heaven is like unto treasure hid in a field; the which when a man hath found, he hideth, and for joy thereof goeth and selleth all that he hath, and buyeth that field. Again, the kingdom of heaven is like unto a merchant man, seeking goodly pearls: Who, when he had found one pearl of great price, went and sold all that he had, and bought it."

What are the results of this treasure hunt? Our reward for seeking the Lord with all our heart gives us joy. Verse fifty-two describes this even more in-depth: *"Then said he unto them, Therefore every scribe which is instructed unto the kingdom of heaven is like unto a man that is an householder, which bringeth forth out of his treasure things new and old."* This is not just a joy to hold onto; this is a lifestyle of learning and teaching others about the treasures that only can be found by living for the Lord. Our salvation and then subsequent service in the kingdom of

God should be so precious that not even a beautiful, expensive pearl could compare in value.

Too many times, we get distracted by the wealth of the world, that corruptible treasure, that we do not seek out the incorruptible treasure. Matthew 6:19-21, *"Lay not up for yourselves treasures upon earth, where moth and rust doth corrupt, and where thieves break through and steal: But lay up for yourselves treasures in heaven, where neither moth nor rust doth corrupt, and where thieves do not break through nor steal: For where your treasure is, there will your heart be also.*

George Muller is reported to have said that when he found Christ, he had found the treasure that he had been seeking for all his life. True treasure seekers are so consumed with finding treasure that nothing can deter them in their quest. Their whole heart is in the hunt to obtain the ultimate prize. Our hidden treasure is described right here in Colossians 2:2-3, *"That their hearts might be comforted, being knit together in love, and unto all riches of the full assurance of understanding, to the acknowledgement of the mystery of God, and of the Father, and of Christ; In whom are hid all the treasures of wisdom and knowledge."*

What treasure are you searching for?

Finders Keepers

"Wherewithal shall a young man cleanse his way? by taking heed thereto according to thy word. With my whole heart have I sought thee: O let me not wander from thy commandments. Thy word have I hid in mine heart, that I might not sin against thee. Blessed art thou, O LORD: teach me thy statutes. With my lips have I declared all the judgments of thy mouth. I have rejoiced in the way of thy testimonies, as much as in all riches. I will meditate in thy precepts, and have respect unto thy ways. I will delight myself in thy statutes: I will not forget thy word." Psalm 119:9-16

Searching for treasure in the Word of God goes beyond finding just a nugget in a verse here and there. When you find a verse that speaks to you, look at the surrounding verses. For example, verse eleven tells us to hide God's Word in our hearts, but the surrounding verses explain why this is necessary and the result of this. Verse fourteen emphasizes how keeping what you have found in God's Word in your heart leads to rejoicing as if you had found a wealth of riches.

Looking at this passage again, you see the writer says, *"With my whole heart have I sought thee..."* When you seek the Lord with your whole heart, you will find treasure worth keeping. We have eight verses written here for our benefit, just a small glimpse of the treasure that you can find in the Word of God.

We hunt for treasure, hunt for houses, hunt for our keys, hunt for a job, hunt for a spouse, and maybe even hunt for food. However, it would be fair to say that too many of God's children do not hunt for treasure in His Word. The riches of God's Word is much more than we can place a monetary value on. As we read previously, the kingdom of God is like a pearl of great price.

Have you considered keeping God's Word in your heart as a treasure?

As I read this passage through, verse fourteen reminds us that once we have hidden the treasure of God's Word in our hearts, we will rejoice in following the guidance and way of His testimonies. Do you notice how treasure hunting in Scripture leads to collecting and then applying those jewels to our lives?

Read it again: *"I have rejoiced in the way of thy testimonies, as much as in all riches."* What makes you rejoice? Is it from the Word of God or the world of fool's gold?

What do you delight in? The word "delight" means to have great joy and pleasure; what you love most is what will delight you. I love the words used in this passage because as I delight (love and find pleasure) in the Word of God and then apply it to my life, it will cause me to rejoice greatly.

Every time I look at this passage, I see new nuggets to meditate upon. However, with daily study of God's Word it will be like opening a treasure chest and finding it full of gems, each one significant in its value and beauty, while collectively adding to the value of the entire chest. Just like that attitude of "finders keepers," we need to be seeking the Lord with our whole hearts and keeping His statutes, judgments, testimonies, and precepts in our hearts and letting them shine forth like treasured jewels.

Open the treasure chest of God's Word and see what great jewels He has for you today. Delight yourself also in the Lord, and He will give you the desires of your heart. Let's go on a treasure hunt. Are you ready? Remember, it's Finders, Keepers!

A Peculiar Treasure

Now therefore, if ye will obey my voice indeed, and keep my covenant, then ye shall be a peculiar treasure unto me above all people: for all the earth is mine: And ye shall be unto me a kingdom of priests, and an holy nation. These are the words which thou shalt speak unto the children of Israel. Exodus 19:5-6.

The Word of God uses such picturesque terms that you can visualize what it is saying. Here, in this passage, the Lord is speaking to Moses in the mountain, reminding him of all that He had done for him and the people of Israel. He tells Moses to tell the people, *"Now therefore, if ye will obey my voice indeed, and keep my covenant, then ye shall be a peculiar treasure unto me above all people: for all the earth is mine:"*

God owns the cattle on a thousand hills, the entire earth, and all creation belongs to Him, yet He calls His people a peculiar treasure. Not just any treasure, but a peculiar one. My dictionary defines this word as strange, odd, unusual, or particular and special. When I look at this word I decided to see where else it was used in the Bible. Deuteronomy 14:2, *"For thou art an holy people unto the LORD thy God, and the LORD hath chosen thee to be a peculiar people unto himself, above all the nations that are upon the earth."* This is reiterated in Deuteronomy 26:18. The children of Israel were a special, chosen people. Does this apply to us, or just to those born into the house of Israel?

When we look in the New Testament, we read in Titus 2:13-14, *"Looking for that blessed hope, and the glorious appearing of the great God and our Saviour Jesus Christ; Who gave himself for us, that he might redeem us from all iniquity, and purify unto himself a peculiar people, zealous of good works."* This is directed to the church, to blood-bought children of God. This is also confirmed in 1 Peter 2:9, *"But ye are a chosen generation, a royal priesthood, an holy nation, a peculiar people; that ye should shew forth the praises of him who hath called you out of darkness into his marvellous light:"*

Read those verses again, my fellow treasure hunter; we are HIS treasure. He placed such value on us to redeem us, to purify us, to make us His peculiar treasure. Look how that great hero and example of faith, Job, says so eloquently in Job 23:10, *"But he knoweth the way that I take: when he hath tried me, I shall come forth as gold."* You are special. You are chosen, even if you have some rough edges. He will always polish you and shape you into His peculiar treasure.

As it says in 1 Peter 1:7-9, *"That the trial of your faith, being much more precious than of gold that perisheth, though it be tried with fire, might be found unto praise and honour and glory at the appearing of Jesus Christ: Whom having not seen, ye love; in whom, though now ye see him not, yet believing, ye rejoice with joy unspeakable and full of glory: Receiving the end of your faith, even the salvation of your souls."*

He placed such value upon you. Do you treasure your time with your Creator, your Refiner? May you show that you treasure Him as you keep His commandments and show forth His praises who hath called you out of darkness into the marvelous light. May you show that you treasure Him as you keep His commandments and show forth His praises Who hath called you out of darkness into the marvelous light.

Heart's Treasure

Matthew 12:35, *"A good man out of the good treasure of the heart bringeth forth good things: and an evil man out of the evil treasure bringeth forth evil things."*

Our hearts hold treasure, according to this verse! We often think about looking for treasure outside of ourselves when we really need to be looking at what is held within our hearts. We get so consumed with gaining material wealth and power when the greatest power and wealth is what we hold in our hearts.

What is this treasure that we hold inside of us? This verse says that familiar adage "what goes in, must come out." We will always be able to tell what sort of person we are and what sort of treasure is in our heart by what our mouth proclaims. Wait, where does Scripture say that? Let's look at the verse right before this one. Verse thirty-four declares, *"O generation of vipers, how can ye, being evil, speak good things? For out of the abundance of the heart the mouth speaketh."*

You have treasure in your heart, but it could be evil, cursed treasure, or it could be good, profitable treasure. We have treasure of one sort or the other, but how do we make sure that we have only good treasure in our heart? Let's look at what one of the writers from the beautiful treasure chest of Psalms tells us to do. Psalm 139:23-24, *"Search me, O God, and know my heart: try me, and know my thoughts: And see if there be any wicked way in me, and lead me in the way everlasting."*

Here we see that our hearts and our minds are completely intertwined with each other. In order to have good treasure in our heart, we need to have a renewed mind that only comes from having our minds transformed through Jesus Christ. Our thoughts are so powerful; we need to treat them as if they are treasure. In fact, they are, but according to our key verse, it is going to be either good or evil treasure.

As redeemed children of God, we have the power of Christ living inside of us. We have the most amazing Treasure of all, the Holy Spirit. Only He can change our trash to treasure. A treasured passage in 2 Corinthians 4 comes to mind. Let's look at just a couple of the verses as they pertain to our thoughts here. Verses six and seven tell us, *"For God, who commanded the light to shine out of darkness, hath shined in our hearts, to give the light of the knowledge of the glory of God in the face of Jesus Christ.*

But we have this treasure in earthen vessels, that the excellency of the power may be of God, and not of us."

You, my dear reader, are full of treasure. But is it being used for the glory of God or the glittery fleshpots of the world? It will be so easy to tell by what you say and how you live. Let every thought be good treasure and not evil.

That's Rich

Colossians 3:1-3, *"If ye then be risen with Christ, seek those things which are above, where Christ sitteth on the right hand of God. Set your affection on things above, not on things on the earth. For ye are dead, and your life is hid with Christ in God."*

What are you looking for? Is it trash or treasure in the realm of God's definition? Your life is a treasure hidden in Christ; it's time to seek out what makes us rich in the eternal economy. What could possibly make us rich and capture our attention and affection so completely? Verses fifteen through seventeen give us the answer to this question. *"And let the peace of God rule in your hearts, to the which also ye are called in one body; and be ye thankful. Let the word of Christ dwell in you richly in all wisdom; teaching and admonishing one another in psalms and hymns and spiritual songs, singing with grace in your hearts to the Lord. And whatsoever ye do in word or deed, do all in the name of the Lord Jesus, giving thanks to God and the Father by him."*

Did you catch those words that are full of eternal wealth and treasure? Let the peace of God rule in your hearts… Jesus is our King, so His peace is to rule us. What an amazing sense of security and protection this displays. If this wasn't enough, it goes on to remind us to let the Word of Christ, the holy Scriptures of God, dwell in us – richly! We are rich! Rich in faith and hope and love through the peace of God that rules in our hearts and the Word of God that dwells in us! How do you know if you are rich?

It will burst forth out of you with how you teach others, how you encourage and instruct and correct others, not just in what you say, but also in what you sing! Music is a treasure trove

17

that wells up in our very innermost being and bursts forth. Is there a song of praise on your lips each day?

Even being clad in the most luxurious garments this world can offer is no match for the beauty and majesty of the riches that a Christian possesses with the Holy Scriptures hidden in our hearts, the peace of God ruling over us, and the songs of worship and praise dripping off our lips like heavenly jewels. When you set your affection on things above, not on things on the earth, you, too, will be rich beyond compare. It really boils down to what do you consider treasure.

Oh, my friend, you can be rich beyond your wildest dreams when you dig for eternal treasure in the rich mercies of God. You will never come to the end of His wealth or go bankrupt in His economy. Now, that, my friend, is rich!

Ship Mates

Imagine that you are on the crew of an expeditionary team searching for treasure. Maybe you are at sea or trekking through dangerous terrain, all in the hopes of finding that purported treasure. There will always be a leader, someone who takes charge and delegates, but that leader is only as good as those who choose to follow.

Sometimes, you may be in that leadership role, and you must depend on those around you to help you carry out the tasks that you have been allotted to perform. Other times, you may be part of that trusty crew that rallies in support of their leader accomplishing great feats together. It is much the same in the hunt for spiritual treasure.

However, like stories of lore, there is too often mutiny in the ranks. We do not like who the leader is, or we get in fights with other members of the team or crew. Rarely does such an expedition succeed when there is mutiny. Carnage, death, and destruction are all that is found when teamwork fails.

Repeatedly, we see through Scripture that we are all to work together with our varied talents and skills to produce treasure for the kingdom of God. What does this look like in our current perspective? This teamwork is best defined as fellowship. Fellowship, in itself, is a treasure that we must value and keep. Fellowship with our Leader, the Lord Jesus Christ, and fellowship with our fellow crew mates, like-minded believers.

What does Scripture say about this fellowship, this treasure-seeking crew? 1 John 1:6-7, *"If we say that we have fellowship with him, and walk in darkness, we lie, and do not the truth: But if we walk in the light, as he is in the light, we have fellowship one with another, and the blood of Jesus Christ his Son cleanseth us from all sin."*

When we have true fellowship with our Captain, the Lord Jesus Christ, we will then have fellowship with one another. Are you feeling like you are doing things all by yourself or that there is no one to help you as you try to live for the Lord? Look to your Captain for help, and He will send the crew that will help and strengthen you as you fellowship together in the work of His kingdom.

Do you consider fellowship with other believers a treasure to seek and find?

Timeless Treasure

Scripture is our treasure chest for those timeless jewels that will last through all eternity. What you might consider the greatest treasure in this whole earthly realm does not compare to even just one promise from God. There was a book that was gifted to me that listed the well-known promises in Scripture. I always considered the book too small to hold every promise of God.

As I look through book titles on the shelves near me, I see titles that use the word treasure to describe the value of what that literary work might contain. Songs of praise, volumes on prayer, all these are indeed treasures. However, these would not be considered treasure if God had not kept even one of His promises. We would no longer consider praising Him or winging our prayers to Him; we would not be able to trust God to be God.

The Bible records God's first promise is of the Messiah as Savior, and the last recorded promise is of the return of that Messiah as King. According to one account, there are 3,573 promises in the Bible. Look at the digits in that number, it starts with the number for Trinity, then comes the number for grace, followed by the number for perfection and completion, and ending again with the number of the Trinity. You may consider this just a far-flung flight of fantasy, but I see a clear presentation of the Gospel in the sequence of those digits. The Triune God sent grace to us, perfected that work of grace, and will graciously reign for all eternity even after time ceases to exist. We have this promised to us, and God never breaks a promise.

Look at what God says about His promise to David in Psalm 89:34, *"My covenant will I not break, nor alter the thing that is gone out of my lips."* As you hold God's Word in your hands, you are holding a treasure trove of God's promises to you. Which promise is most precious to you today? In a world full of betrayal, broken trust, and disintegrating relationships, we have the promise that He will be with us, He will comfort us, He will strengthen us. You only have to dip into the treasure chest of God's Word to find and hold onto those promises for yourself. Time can never rob us of God's promises; they are timeless treasures.

Romans 11:33-36, *"O the depth of the riches both of the wisdom and knowledge of God! how unsearchable are his judgments, and his ways past finding out! For who hath known the mind of the Lord? or who hath been his counsellor? Or who hath first given to him, and it shall be recompensed unto him again? For of him, and through him, and to him, are all things: to whom be glory for ever. Amen."*

Open your treasured copy of God's Word and search out His promise for you today.

Precious Patience

Patience. This particular fruit from the Holy Spirit is more treasured and valued than many of the others. This is because we have so little of it. This is NOT the fault of the Holy Spirit of God; it is, however, the distinct fact that our hearts and minds are not fertile ground for patience to blossom forth and produce fruit.

Favored passages are quoted and emblazoned on walls and social media accounts, yet the fruition of these words seems to be unattainable or amount to fast-fleeting moments.

Psalm 27:13-14, *"I had fainted, unless I had believed to see the goodness of the Lord in the land of the living. Wait on the Lord: be of good courage, and he shall strengthen thine heart: wait, I say, on the Lord."* The Psalmist knew about waiting upon the Lord, serving Him, following Him, so being patient was precious to him.

Isaiah 40:31, *"But they that wait upon the Lord shall renew their strength; they shall mount up with wings as eagles; they shall run, and not be weary; and they shall walk, and not faint."*

These verses emphasize the result of patience, that is the patience of waiting upon the Lord. To be still and to know that He is God has resounded almost daily within my heart this year. Unfortunately, pressure and stress seem to make it feel as if we are running out of time, that God is taking too long, or a decision has to be made.

We end up getting impatient, stressed, frustrated, maybe even angry, when all the time, God is offering strength, courage, and endurance when we wait on His way, His will, His when, His where, and His what, maybe even His why. One of my favorite authors says patience is of great spiritual value because it is the source of our primary spiritual strength.

Is patience precious to you because you don't have any, or is it precious because you are allowing God to work in your life, strengthening and growing you as you serve Him?

What sort of things do you need patience for that only God can give you?

Valuable Vessels

When we collect treasure, we don't just look at it one time; we are always eager to view it and handle it. The same concept and reaction need to be even more prevalent with Scripture. Although we have mentioned the following verses in a previous section, they are so full of treasure that I want to devote more time to basking in their value.

Open your treasured Scripture to 2 Corinthians 4:6-11 and let's look at the valuables found therein. We touched briefly on this passage in an earlier treasure hunt but let's search it out to a greater extent. It says, *"For God, who commanded the light to shine out of darkness, hath shined in our hearts, to give the light of the knowledge of the glory of God in the face of Jesus Christ. But we have this treasure in earthen vessels, that the excellency of the power may be of God, and not of us. We are troubled on every side, yet not distressed; we are perplexed, but not in despair; Persecuted, but not forsaken; cast down, but not destroyed; Always bearing about in the body the dying of the Lord Jesus, that the life also of Jesus might be made manifest in our body. For we which live are always delivered unto death for Jesus' sake, that the life also of Jesus might be made manifest in our mortal flesh."*

I always concentrated on the encouragement these verses promised and sought comfort in the fact that, no matter what happens, I can make it through with the power of Jesus Christ. However, I really did not pay attention to the first part of these verses. We have this treasure in earthen vessels... There is no treasure without the power, nay the excellency of the power of God. The treasure, however, is Christ in us, the hope of glory! We are earthen vessels that contain Treasure given to us through salvation.

You are the vessel that God chooses to put His Treasure in; He tells us all throughout Scripture how much He loves us and places value on our lives. Not because of who we are, but because of Who He is and Whose we are. Soak that in for a few minutes. God has chosen you to be a vessel for His power, His message, His life, His light to be viewed in us to all those who see us.

Maybe you say, "I don't feel like a treasure, much less a valuable vessel." Let's look at why God chose YOU to be His vessel of value.

Ephesians 1:1-7, *"And you hath he quickened, who were dead in trespasses and sins; Wherein in time past ye walked according to the course of this world, according to the prince of the power of the air, the spirit that now worketh in the children of disobedience: Among whom also we all had our conversation in times past in the lusts of our flesh, fulfilling the desires of the flesh and of the mind; and were by nature the children of wrath, even as others. But God, who is rich in mercy, for his great love wherewith he loved us, Even when we were dead in sins, hath quickened us together with Christ, (by grace ye are saved;) And hath raised us up together, and made us sit together in heavenly places in Christ Jesus: That in the ages to come he might shew the exceeding riches of his grace in his kindness toward us through Christ Jesus."*

God is rich in mercy; He loves us, makes us alive in and through His salvation, and has saved us a seat in Heaven! You, dear saint, are a valuable vessel!

Treasure Trove

Where do you hunt for treasure? Historically, it is often buried or lost at sea; it takes great effort and time to search and find the treasure you are hunting for. It becomes the singular focus of the hunter to obtain his prize. Why are we not singularly focused on hunting for treasures for the heart in the same way?

What sort of tools help with this treasure hunt? God uses His Word first and foremost for that is the treasure that I am seeking. In addition, He gives me devotionals, messages in sermons, and other tools through godly friends to aid in my treasure hunt. Do you take sermon notes? As I looked through my sermon notes from the last year, I found so many of them spoke exactly to the sort of treasures I need to have in my heart.

When you find treasure, you observe it, you study it, you handle it carefully, inspecting it and ascertaining its value. This exact same reaction is necessary for the treasure we find in God's Word. 2 Timothy 2:15 says, *"Study to shew thyself approved unto God, a workman that needeth not to be ashamed, rightly dividing the word of truth."* Remember, you are the vessel that holds treasure, but what sort of treasure is in your vessel? Is it God's Word or worldly trinkets?

Take out the treasure that you are holding in your heart, study it, and inspect it. Is it of any eternal value? If you took this treasure that you are keeping in your heart and had it appraised by the spiritual Appraiser, the Holy Spirit, how would it meet His "gold standard"?

Isaiah 34:16, *"Seek ye out of the book of the LORD, and read..."* When you read, you will find treasure like Isaiah 45:3, *"And I will give thee the treasures of darkness, and hidden riches of secret places, that thou mayest know that I, the Lord, which call thee by thy name, am the God of Israel."*

My friend sent me that passage just this morning as she knows that I am on a Scripture treasure hunt. Surround yourselves with friends who encourage you in your own treasure hunt. Your heart is seeking real treasure which can only be found in God's Word.

Let's go on a treasure hunt and see what treasures and hidden riches God will reveal to us for our good and His glory.

Sacred Sanctuary

Matthew 6:21, *"For where your treasure is, there will your heart be also."* This verse is the solid foundation for this entire devotional. The Bible tells us in 1 Corinthians 6:19-20 that our body is the temple of the Holy Ghost, so if our body is His temple, our hearts are His throne room! What goes into your mind will then enter into your heart. Is your heart a sacred sanctuary for the Holy Spirit of God to dwell in?

Sacred means set apart unto a holy purpose, and sanctuary is a refuge, a place of safety. Your heart is to be a place of refuge set apart unto holiness. We often hear about how we are to take care of our bodies, but how do we take care of our hearts? We have touched on many verses in previous treasure hunts that would help in our search for making our hearts a sacred sanctuary. Which one has come to mind as you read that just now? My mind went immediately to Psalm 119:11, *"Thy word have I hid in mine heart, that I might not sin against thee."*

What's in your heart? As you enter a throne room of royalty, you will often sense an air of expectancy but also a reverential hush. Your heart should be eagerly expecting to hear the voice of God speaking to you through His Word, the Bible. However, you need to be still and hushed so that you can hear what He has to say from His throne directly to you. Psalm 46:10 is so often quoted, but rarely is it obeyed. *"Be still, and know that I am God: I will be exalted among the heathen, I will be exalted in the earth."* Still your heart, wait expectantly for His Word to speak with you, hide it in your heart, and commune with God, your King.

Psalm 119:112, *"I have inclined mine heart to perform thy statutes alway, even unto the end."* Our hearts are His throne room; we listen to Him, but we need to take it a step further and obey what He tells us.

A sacred sanctuary, can you picture it? Images of grand cathedrals come to mind with sunbeams casting a prismatic hue through stained glass windows onto the inhabitants gathered within its hallowed halls. We use beautiful words to describe beautiful places, but what about our hearts?

Exodus 25:8, *"And let them make me a sanctuary; that I may dwell among them."* Hebrews 10:16, *"This is the covenant that I will make with them after those days, saith the Lord, I will put my laws into their hearts, and in their minds will I write them;"*

What's in your heart today? Will you pray that the Lord will make you His sanctuary?

Wondrous Walk

A walk is made of steps, it has a destination, an ending point. Many times, our life with Christ is illustrated by a walk. This is found repeatedly in Scripture, for example, Psalm 119:45, *"And I will walk at liberty: for I seek thy precepts."* Where is your walk going? Revelation 21:24 says, *"And the nations of them which are saved shall walk in the light of it: and the kings of the earth do bring their glory and honour into it."* This is referring to the New Jerusalem. When we walk in the precepts of God through the liberty of His grace, we will reach the end of our journey here on this earth, but then, we will resume our walk in celestial surroundings. Now, that, my friends, is a wondrous walk.

What makes a wondrous walk? The destination, the direction, and the delight.

Proverbs 3:6, *"In all thy ways acknowledge him, and he shall direct thy paths."* Where are you going? Psalm 119:59, *"I thought on my ways, and turned my feet unto thy testimonies."* Ponder your direction and your destination; turn your feet if they are taking you anywhere but to that Heavenly Home. Maybe you are saved, but you are not walking with the Lord. We use those phrases so often that we no longer picture what they actually mean. The Lord is walking with you after you are saved, very literally in the spiritual realm. How else will we be able to walk the distance, through difficulties, death, or dark times if He is not with us?

Your walk should be different from those who are not walking with Jesus. The book of 2 John only has one chapter, but verse four is so powerful to keep as a goal. *"I rejoiced greatly that I found of thy children walking in truth, as we have received a commandment from the Father."*

Our walk with the Lord will have a great influence on those around us. It will deeply affect our children and family one way or the other.

A wondrous walk is one that is full of delight. Psalm 119:35, *"Make me to go in the path of thy commandments; for therein do I delight."* Psalm 23 illustrates this so beautifully. *"The Lord is my shepherd; I shall not want. He maketh me to lie down in green pastures: he leadeth me beside the still waters. He restoreth my soul: he leadeth me in the paths of righteousness for his name's sake. Yea, though I walk through the valley of the shadow of death, I will fear no evil: for thou art with me; thy rod and thy staff they comfort me. Thou preparest a table before me in the presence of mine enemies: thou anointest my head with oil; my cup runneth over. Surely goodness and mercy shall follow me all the days of my life: and I will dwell in the house of the Lord for ever."*

This Psalm has a path laid out for the one who chooses to walk on it. It says we are led by still waters; we are also led in the paths of righteousness for His Name's sake, even if those paths lead us through a valley near death's shadow. This tells me that the Shepherd is guiding me on this walk and choosing the places along the way that are best for me to go. He is leading, and I am to follow faithfully and trust His direction. How do we know we can trust Him? Because it states right here that He restores our soul; we do not need to fear evil; He will comfort us. He will provide for us and bless us along the way for our faithful following. If you keep looking over your shoulder to see where He has brought you from, you will notice goodness and mercy have followed you. What a delight there is to experience and treasure when we walk with our Shepherd, following His path of righteousness.

So much more could be noted therein about walking with the Lord. Why not study for yourself those who walked with God and the results of their walks, Adam and Eve, Enoch, the disciples, and even those on the road to Emmaus, just to name a few.

Pernicious Pirates

Every treasure collector has an enemy: a pirate seeking to steal and pilfer for their own gain and your loss. My current nemesis is a time stealer! Our current society is obsessed with social media platforms, binge watching shows and movies, and/or playing video games. Electronic entertainment has become a real pirate of our time with God. Remember that which we put into our minds gets collected into our hearts. Whatever we spend the most time on is usually what we treasure the most.

Distractions are pernicious pirates, and boy, do we fall prey to their traps. Galatians 5:7 asks this question of us: *"Ye did run well; who did hinder you that ye should not obey the truth?"* Hinder can mean to get in the way, to keep you from your goal, to distract, to cause you to stumble and fall.

In days past, the pirates were feared, but also great lengths were made to be protected against the pirates and their dreaded attacks on precious possessions. Today, we think they make great characters in movies, we long to find their stolen, buried treasure, but we do not dread them. Their thieving ways are no longer vilified but heralded and emulated. We treat time thieves the same way; we exalt those distractions and deeds that take precious time away from us.

Jesus is to be our treasure; time spent with Him is above value. When we look at it this way, those other pursuits and distractions should have no sway over us. Matthew 22:37, *"Jesus said unto him, Thou shalt love the Lord thy God with all thy heart, and with all thy soul, and with all thy mind."* Sadly, we do not treasure the Lord in this way, with all that we are and have. Instead, we are like the Israelites in the book of Judges. Let's read what Judges 2 says about the Israelites and their pursuit of ungodly delights.

Take time to read this whole chapter; we have much with which we can compare ourselves with those Israelites. Verses ten through twelve caught my eye. *"And also all that generation were gathered unto their fathers: and there arose another generation after them, which knew not the LORD, nor yet the works which he had done for Israel. And the children of Israel did evil in the sight of the Lord, and served Baalim: And they forsook the Lord God of their fathers, which brought them out of the land of Egypt, and followed other gods, of the gods of the people that were round about them, and bowed themselves unto them, and provoked the Lord to anger."*

Did you catch it? There arose another generation that knew not the Lord nor what He had done for Israel. How was that possible?

The next generation is already with us. What has their attention, the distractions and destruction of the world, or the works that God has done in your life that you are proclaiming to them?

Treacherous Traps

Any treasure seeker knows that the way to the treasure is fraught with treacherous traps. Many of these traps are in the form of temptations that will sidetrack us from our ultimate goal. We are promised that we have the victory over these temptations.

Romans 8:35-39 names the deadly traps and yet shows us that because of Christ's love for us, we are able to survive and overcome these deadly snares. Let's read it together and absorb this nugget of precious help and hope.

"Who shall separate us from the love of Christ? Shall tribulation, or distress, or persecution, or famine, or nakedness, or peril, or sword? As it is written, For thy sake we are killed all the day long; we are accounted as sheep for the slaughter. Nay, in all these things we are more than conquerors through him that loved us. For I am persuaded, that neither death, nor life, nor angels, nor principalities, nor powers, nor things present, nor things to come, Nor height, nor depth, nor any other creature, shall be able to separate us from the love of God, which is in Christ Jesus our Lord."

Maybe you think that this all sounds grand but that the actual victory just does not seem to happen. Instead, the temptations and defeat just overwhelm you. The next passage really made an impact on how the temptations that beset me are not too much for the Avenger of our souls to defeat.

1 Corinthians 10:13 states, *"There hath no temptation taken you but such as is common to man: but God is faithful, who will not suffer you to tempted above that ye are able; but will with the temptation also make a way to escape, that ye may be able to bear it."*

These verses give perseverance to the saint! He loves us, He gives us victory because of His love and faithfulness, and He gives us a way to escape each and every temptation. We can fight and forge ahead every day in victory!

What is trying to trap you today? Will you trust God to provide the way of escape for you to be able to have the victory?

Real Riches

What are the real riches that we are to be collecting in our hearts? James 1 puts a spotlight on a few of these valuable gems. Verse two starts with, *"My brethren, count it all joy when ye fall into divers temptations; Knowing this, that the trying of your faith worketh patience."* Rarely do we ever equate joy with many varied and seemingly endless trials and temptations. In a previous study, we looked at the concept that we will face trials and trouble on every side. We get into the mindset that life should be clear sailing and we can have whatever we want when we want it. This is so misleading and deceptive to the Christian who is suddenly overwhelmed by life. The very word LIFE has a huge "IF" in the middle of it! How, then, do we find value in these trials? Let's look at verse four of this same chapter: *"But let patience have her perfect work, that ye may be perfect and entire, wanting nothing."* Now, patience is something that is sorely lacking and so desperately necessary to endure trials. It's the trying of your faith that worketh patience, NOT the trying of your patience! Verse five through eight continues this same thought: *"If any of you lack wisdom, let him ask of God, that giveth to all men liberally, and upbraideth not; and it shall be given him. But let him ask in faith, nothing wavering. For he that wavereth is like a wave of the sea driven with the wind and tossed. For let not that man think that he shall receive any thing of the Lord. A double minded man is unstable in all his ways."*

The only way to collect patience and wisdom from God is to have faith in God to give it to you when and as you need it. Are you feeling tossed about and overwhelmed by the seas that have grown stormy? Even the great cruise ships encounter hurricanes out on the oceans of this world. You have to ride out the storm with faith, wisdom, and patience.

The first chapter in James could end there, and it would be plenty for us to work on, however, it continues. Verses nine through twelve expand on this faithful perseverance by reminding us that life is short, and its value is not in earthly riches that will fade away. Let's look at this part of the chapter: Verse nine, *"Let the brother of low degree rejoice in that he is exalted:"* admonishes us to stay humble in our service to our Lord; He will exalt you as He deems fit. My friend, heed well the warning given in verses ten through eleven and do not be blinded by worldly wealth or fame. *"But the rich, in that he is made low: because as the flower of the grass he shall pass away. For the sun is no sooner risen with a burning heat, but it withereth the grass, and the flower thereof falleth, and the grace of the fashion of it perisheth: so also shall the rich man fade away in his ways."*

The real riches are found in verse twelve: *"Blessed is the man that endureth temptation: for when he is tried, he shall receive the crown of life, which the Lord hath promised to them that love him."*

Do you have fools' gold, or faith's golden treasure, the crown of life?

Treasures Unseen

A well-loved song often sung in our churches in this region has this phrase that caught my attention as this devotional was being developed. Treasures unseen, what could that possibly mean? What comes to your mind when you think of unseen treasure? Further down in the song, it answers this question with "The secret to hidden possessions is to love Him and serve Him every day." This song reminds us that there is joy in serving Jesus.

A popular restaurant serves its customers with a delightful phrase, "My Pleasure," and it always makes the customer feel treasured just for ordering at their establishment. Is the Lord delighted with your service to Him? Do you wake up each morning and ask Him how you may serve Him today? Is it your pleasure to serve the Lord?

"Bless the LORD, O my soul: and all that is within me, bless his holy name. Bless the LORD, O my soul, and forget not all his benefits: Who forgiveth all thine iniquities; who healeth all thy diseases; Who redeemeth thy life from destruction; who crowneth thee with lovingkindness and tender mercies; Who satisfieth thy mouth with good things; so that thy youth is renewed like the eagle's." Psalms 103:1-5

As you read this Psalm through, you will see many treasures unseen which results in our service to the King of kings. The first is *bless the Lord*, but how do you bless the Lord? Well, what makes Him happy? Your faithful service and obedience are paramount of course, but here it says by not forgetting all His benefits. What are these benefits, these treasures? This Psalm proceeds to list them: forgiveness of iniquities, healing of diseases, redemption of life from destruction. But wait, what is that benefit, that treasure in verse four? *"Who crowneth thee with lovingkindness and tender mercies. "* That sounds like treasure to me! Are you wearing that crown today? In a future devotional entry, we will talk about the crowns that we are given in our Christian life, but this one is rarely mentioned as one of them.

You have been crowned with lovingkindness and tender mercies. Are you wearing this crown today as a symbol of your delight to do His will? Let's look at further treasures in serving the Lord as found in Psalm 112:1-3, *"Praise ye the LORD. Blessed is the man that feareth the LORD, that delighteth greatly in his commandments. His seed shall be mighty upon earth: the generation of the upright shall be blessed. Wealth and riches shall be in his house: and his righteousness endureth for ever. "*

What treasures do you notice here that might have been unseen to you the previous times you read through the Psalms? Those who delight greatly in His commands shall be blessed; they shall have wealth and riches. Now we could say this might apply to earthly treasure, but preferably to heavenly treasure found in the house of God. These are the treasures unseen that are found by those who delight in doing the will of their heavenly Father.

In the space below, list the ways you want to delight in serving the Lord this week:

_____

_____

_____

_____

_____

Unexpected Treasure

Treasure is mentioned around seventy-seven times in the Bible, however, not every mention of treasure is of the usual gold and silver variety. *"When he uttereth his voice, there is a multitude of waters in the heavens, and he causeth the vapours to ascend from the ends of the earth; he maketh lightnings with rain, and bringeth forth the wind out of his treasures."* Jeremiah 10:13.

This very statement is repeated again in Jeremiah 51:16. Why would God want us to know that wind is part of His treasure? God's treasure house, His storehouse, contains wind! Wind is used throughout Scripture in various ways. It's a powerful tool in the hands of the Creator God. We do not often equate wind with treasure.

What else does God keep in His storehouse of treasures?

"And of Joseph he said, Blessed of the LORD be his land, for the precious things of heaven, for the dew, and for the deep that coucheth beneath, And for the precious fruits brought forth by the sun, and for the precious things put forth by the moon, And for the chief things of the ancient mountains, and for the precious things of the lasting hills, And for the precious things of the earth and fulness thereof, and for the good will of him that dwelt in the bush:" Deuteronomy 33:13-16.

The precious things are listed as things from nature, from creation. If something is precious, then it has value and worth. We do not often expect God's creation to be on the same standard of value as geological treasures. Again, our minds are so narrow that we miss out on unexpected treasures because we do not equate them with the same level of value that God does. You know, we do that with people as well. Our perception of that person is based on how much we value them, not how precious they are in God's eyes.

In the book of Job, the Lord is answering Job, and as you read chapter thirty-eight with such vivid description, you will find these verses:

"Hast thou entered into the treasures of the snow? or hast thou seen the treasures of the hail, Which I have reserved against the time of trouble, against the day of battle and war?" Job 38:22-23.

God keeps snow and hail in His treasure house, the hail He has reserved for the day of battle. When you read of the judgments in Revelation, you will see that hail is used. Hail was used in Egypt as well, and yet, because it comes from the King, our Creator, it is treasure to Him.

Snow, dew, wind, hail, darkness, light, and so many more are all named as treasures in the storehouse of God. If God places value on these parts of His creation, how much more valuable are we as His children?

Right now, take a moment and consider the lilies of the field, the still waters, the soft summer breeze, and thank the Lord for showing you a glimpse of the unexpected treasure in His storehouse.

Treasure House

Treasure is so often mentioned in the Bible that it amazes me how we do not seem to pay much attention to it. Have you become so dismissive of what God values? Let's look at our text in Ezra 1 and read all eleven verses: *"Now in the first year of Cyrus king of Persia, that the word of the LORD by the mouth of Jeremiah might be fulfilled, the LORD stirred up the spirit of Cyrus king of Persia, that he made a proclamation throughout all his kingdom, and put it also in writing, saying, Thus saith Cyrus king of Persia, The LORD God of heaven hath given me all the kingdoms of the earth; and he hath charged me to build him an house at Jerusalem, which is in Judah. Who is there among you of all his people? his God be with him, and let him go up to Jerusalem, which is in Judah, and build the house of the LORD God of Israel, (he is the God,) which is in Jerusalem. And whosoever remaineth in any place where he sojourneth, let the men of his place help him with silver, and with gold, and with goods, and with beasts, beside the freewill offering for the house of God that is in Jerusalem. Then rose up the chief of the fathers of Judah and Benjamin, and the priests, and the Levites, with all them whose spirit God had raised, to go up to build the house of the LORD which is in Jerusalem. And all they that were about them strengthened their hands with vessels of silver, with gold, with goods, and with beasts, and with precious things, beside all that was willingly offered. Also Cyrus the king brought forth the vessels of the house of the LORD, which Nebuchadnezzar had brought forth out of Jerusalem, and had put them in the house of his gods; Even those did Cyrus king of Persia bring forth by the hand of Mithredath the treasurer, and numbered them unto Sheshbazzar, the prince of Judah. And this is the number of them: thirty chargers of gold, a thousand chargers of silver, nine and twenty knives, Thirty basons of gold, silver basons of a second sort four hundred and ten, and other vessels a thousand. All the vessels of gold and of silver were five thousand and four hundred. All these did Sheshbazzar bring up with them of the captivity that were brought up from Babylon unto Jerusalem."*

Did you notice the treasure that was described in this passage? Not only were they going to return all the treasure that had been captured, but the pagan king was going to add more treasure to be put into the house of God (He is THE God). As the items of treasure were listed, the phrases *house of God* and they *willingly offered* caught my attention. As you read through the book of Ezra, you'll see various things were stored in treasure houses, including records and letters! What is stored in your treasure house? Do you treasure the house of God? There is much treasure in His treasure house, but they also willingly offered more than what they were already returning to their rightful place.

While reading through the Bible, many books were written in the same time frame with varying perspectives on what transpired during that time. If you were to read the book of Nehemiah alongside Ezra, you would see the specific work and treasure that was also used to rebuild that which had been destroyed. Much treasure was given to rebuild the wall of Jerusalem, the city of God, and then to also rebuild His house. Nehemiah 11:2, *"And the people blessed all the men, that willingly offered themselves to dwell at Jerusalem."* Did you catch that? Men were chosen to serve in the house of God, and they offered themselves willingly, and the people blessed them for their service. This should remind you of the previous devotional entry about "Treasures Unseen." It was their pleasure to serve in the house of God; they were willing to be in charge of what was brought into God's treasure house.

Now you may think that this was just for the people called the Israelites. How does this pertain to us as children of God? Let's look at Romans 12:1, *"I beseech you therefore, brethren, by the mercies of God, that ye present your bodies a living sacrifice, holy, acceptable unto God, which is your reasonable service."* You are God's treasure designed for His treasure house. How do we know this? 1 Corinthians 3:16-17, *"Know ye not that ye are the temple of God, and that the Spirit of God dwelleth in you? If any man defile the temple of God, him shall God destroy; for the temple of God is holy, which temple ye are."* This is repeated again in chapter six verses nineteen through twenty *"What? know ye not that your body is the temple of the Holy Ghost which is in you, which ye have of God, and ye are not your own? For ye are bought with a price: therefore glorify God in your body, and in your spirit, which are God's."*

Soak that in for a minute; you are so treasured by God that He chose to dwell in your redeemed temple and make it His own!

Now it's your turn to store up treasure in God's treasure house. Read the following passages on your own and discover what God treasures for His House.

2 Corinthians 6:16 _____

Revelation 3:12 _____

Revelation 7:15 _____

Revelation 11:1 …measure the temple of God, and the altar, and

_____

Facets of Faith

Gemstones are often considered more beautiful when they have facets. What are facets? The way something is cut so that it has multiple sides or "faces." How would this be illustrated in our faith? What are the many aspects of your faith? Let's put it even simpler; if your faith had a face, what would it be? We have many expressions; how do we express our faith to God, to others, or even to ourselves?

In order to create facets, one had to cut carefully and expertly into the precious stone. Faith is the tool that God uses to carefully bring out the exquisite beauty of His design in us as His precious stones. Malachi 3:17 uses a lovely phrase that catches my attention, *"And they shall be mine, saith the LORD of hosts, in that day when I make up my jewels."* Obviously, it is necessary to read this whole chapter for context, and I really hope you will read it because it's so applicable to what is going on in our day and age. Yet, the lovely phrase, *"When I make up my jewels,"* catches my treasure-hunting eyes. The Master Jeweler, the Designer of crowns and of all things beautiful, is making jewels out of His people. When you look back at the verse before it, you'll understand even more how precious our faith is to God.

Verse sixteen: *"Then they that feared the LORD spake often one to another: and the LORD hearkened, and heard it, and a book of remembrance was written before him for them that feared the LORD, and that thought upon his name."* He treasures our fear, our worship, our reverence, our faith, our witness to others, and our thinking upon His Name. He writes about the faith of His people in His book of remembrance and turns our faith into facets in His Heavenly jewels.

Faith has many facets: saving faith, living faith, sharing faith, abiding faith, strong faith, weak faith, unwavering faith, indwelling faith, growing faith, precious faith, perfect faith, and great faith just to name some. As I looked up some of these, I saw that it was listed under the heading of Scripture nuggets, how applicable that is when we are talking about precious jewels of faith.

2 Peter 1:1 talks about precious faith: *"Simon Peter, a servant and an apostle of Jesus Christ, to them that have obtained like precious faith with us through the righteousness of God and our Saviour Jesus Christ:"* Those who have obtained precious faith. How precious is your faith? Is it a facet being carved into a heavenly jewel?

Let's look at another facet of faith. Strong faith is something we all want to have. How do we get strong faith? Scripture says that the trying of our faith worketh patience… Romans 4:20-22 says this about Abraham, *"He staggered not at the promise of God through unbelief; but was strong in faith, giving glory to God; And being fully persuaded that, what he had promised, he was able also to perform. And therefore it was imputed to him for righteousness."*

I looked up the definition of imputed because it brought back to mind verse sixteen of Malachi 3, that book of remembrance. A common definition of imputed is "a financial term meaning a value assigned to something by inference from the value of the products or processes to which it contributes."

Abraham had strong faith. It was recorded for us, and it was assigned intrinsic value by God. Precious faith and strong faith. Just these two facets of faith are plenty for us to treasure. Maybe there are some other facets of faith that came to your mind.

How do we allow God to cut away the imperfections and create in us a precious jewel? 1 John 5:4-5, *"For whatsoever is born of God overcometh the world: and this is the victory that overcometh the world, even our faith. Who is he that overcometh the world, but he that believeth that Jesus is the Son of God?"*

What sort of faith overcomes the world? It is, my friend, the victorious faith of those who believe that Jesus is the Son of God. And as it states in John 20:31, *"But these are written, that ye might believe that Jesus is the Christ, the Son of God; and that believing ye might have life through his name."*

An in-depth study of the facets of faith is something that every person who is saved by the first facet of faith, believing that only Jesus can save them from their sin, should earnestly pursue. Personally, my studies of faith often led to studies on prayer which would then lead me back to an even deeper study about faith. Hebrews 11:6, *"But without faith it is impossible to please him: for he that cometh to God must believe that he is, and that he is a rewarder of them that diligently seek him."*

Which facet of faith will you begin to study this week?

Rubies, Diamonds, and Pearls, O My!

Listening to our church's weekly broadcast, the title of one of the messages was "Pearls in the Psalms." Immediately, my thoughts ran to the pearl of great price, but pearls of wisdom also came to mind. When I think of pearls in Scripture, I think of pearls of wisdom. The book of Proverbs is usually thought of most often as a book pertaining to wisdom.

Do you think of the books of the Bible as precious gems? As this devotional entry ran through my mind, I thought of Rubies in Ruth, Diamonds in Daniel, and Pearls in Proverbs, but what about Gems in Genesis, Gold in Galatians, Jewels in James, or Silver in Psalms?

Let's go down the precious stone road and see what treasure we can find.

Gems in Genesis: Genesis 15:1, *"After these things the word of the LORD came unto Abram in a vision, saying, Fear not, Abram: I am thy shield, and thy exceeding great reward."* God is our Shield, our Refuge, and our Reward! What treasure!

What gem in Genesis do you value?

_____

Let's find a ruby in Ruth 2:12, *"The LORD recompense thy work, and a full reward be given thee of the LORD God of Israel, under whose wings thou art come to trust."*

Now it's your turn. What ruby in Ruth do you treasure?

_____

Daniel is a book with many diamonds in it. Every chapter in this book is a diamond for me! Diamonds are strong stones formed under severe conditions; we need to have faith as strong as diamonds! I think of Daniel purposing in his heart not to defile himself as found in chapter one verse 8, or the times that he defied pagan decrees and purposefully prayed to God, or the visions of Heaven that he was allowed to see. Maybe your diamond in Daniel is the story of the three men who would not bow to the statue. Their faith in God was as strong as diamonds. What is your diamond from the book of Daniel?

Wisdom is a precious jewel; it is indeed a pearl and beyond value to the one who possesses it. Proverbs 2:1-9 gives us just one such description of the value of wisdom. *"My son, if thou wilt receive my words, and hide my commandments with thee; So that thou incline thine ear unto wisdom, and apply thine heart to understanding; Yea, if thou criest after knowledge, and liftest up thy voice for understanding; If thou seekest her as silver, and searchest for her as for hid treasures; Then shalt thou understand the fear of the LORD, and find the knowledge of God. For the LORD giveth wisdom: out of his mouth cometh knowledge and understanding. He layeth up sound wisdom for the righteous: he is a buckler to them that walk uprightly. He keepeth the paths of judgment, and preserveth the way of his saints. Then shalt thou understand righteousness, and judgment, and equity; yea, every good path."*

Which pearl in Proverbs do you value?

James is also a book of wisdom found in God's Book of Treasures, there is so much to be found in the study of James. Have you studied this book for yourself yet? What jewel in James comes to mind for you?

We have mentioned finding gold in Galatians, did you look for any verse in Galatians to add to your treasure chest?

The book of Psalms is probably the most popular book, just as silver is often the most popular precious metal that is used today. Psalms is a precious book of comfort and confidence in our God in Whom we trust. List some of your treasured Psalms

that you use in your daily walk down the road winding ever
upwards.

_____

_____

_____

_____

_____

Acres of Diamonds

A beautiful song written by Arthur Smith entitled "Acres of Diamonds" has been running through my mind lately. Here is the song:

Acres of Diamonds, mountains of gold, Rivers of silver, jewels untold; All these together, wouldn't buy you or me peace when we're sleeping or a conscience that's free.

A heart that's contented, a satisfied mind, these are the treasures, money can't buy. If you have Jesus, there's more wealth in your soul, than acres of diamonds, mountains of gold.

What a great little song, so full of treasure! Let's open this treasure chest and see what's inside. All the riches of this world cannot compare to what God has in store for His children. All the riches in the world will not buy you peace, a free conscience, contentment, or a satisfied mind. The phrase, "a heart that is contented, a satisfied mind," keeps running around my mind like they are on constant replay.

"But godliness with contentment is great gain. For we brought nothing into this world, and it is certain we can carry nothing out. And having food and raiment let us be therewith content. But they that will be rich fall into temptation and a snare, and into many foolish and hurtful lusts, which drown men in destruction and perdition. For the love of money is the root of all evil: which while some coveted after, they have erred from the faith, and pierced themselves through with many sorrows. But thou, O man of God, flee these things; and follow after righteousness, godliness, faith, love, patience, meekness. Fight the good fight of faith, lay hold on eternal life, whereunto thou art also called, and hast professed a good profession before many witnesses." 1 Timothy 6:6-12.

We need to be rich in faith and hope and love, not in treasures of this world. Be content, be godly, and when Jesus is enough, then you will have a satisfied mind and heart!

2 Corinthians 12:9-10, *"And he said unto me, My grace is sufficient for thee: for my strength is made perfect in weakness. Most gladly therefore will I rather glory in my infirmities, that the power of Christ may rest upon me. Therefore I take pleasure in infirmities, in reproaches, in necessities, in persecutions, in distresses for Christ's sake: for when I am weak, then am I strong."*

What are your thoughts about this? Is Jesus enough for you?

"Let your conversation be without covetousness; and be content with such things as ye have: for he hath said, I will never leave thee, nor forsake thee. So that we may boldly say, The Lord is my helper, and I will not fear what man shall do unto me." Hebrews 13:5-6.

Let your conversation, that is your conduct, as well as your speech, be without coveting, and be content; why is this stated repeatedly? Verse six of Hebrews 13 is such a clear answer, *"so that with bold confidence we can proclaim that the Lord is my helper!"* All the diamonds and wealth of this world is only temporary if you were even to obtain them; what is done for Christ will last throughout all eternity.

What are some of the things that leave you feeling discontented or ruin your peace of mind?

_____

_____

_____

How many lines for writing did you feel like you needed to have to list them all?

Now, these are the very things that are robbing you of your peace and keeping you from trusting God to be your helper!

Colossians 3:15-17 reminds us again how to defeat the pirates that are trying to steal our treasure of peace and contentment.

"And let the peace of God rule in your hearts, to the which also ye are called in one body; and be ye thankful. Let the word of Christ dwell in you richly in all wisdom; teaching and admonishing one another in psalms and hymns and spiritual songs, singing with grace in your hearts to the Lord. And whatsoever ye do in word or deed, do all in the name of the Lord Jesus, giving thanks to God and the Father by him."

Little Treasures

"I don't have much in this world…" Dear friend, it's not about quantity or even dollar amount; it's sometimes the little treasures that mean the most. What would be some little treasures that would still be considered invaluable and priceless? Even the miner knew the value of gold dust!

Little treasures are the little things and opportunities you are given to serve the Lord. Most of these should go unnoticed by the crowd; they are done for the Lord, not public recognition. Are you only serving in church to get recognition by others? Their recognition is your reward, and thus, you miss out on the treasure that you could receive in Heaven when all is done for the glory of God! Value your dedication to God.

"For the kingdom of heaven is as a man travelling into a far country, who called his own servants, and delivered unto them his goods. And unto one he gave five talents, to another two, and to another one; to every man according to his several ability; and straightway took his journey. Then he that had received the five talents went and traded with the same, and made them other five talents. And likewise he that had received two, he also gained other two. But he that had received one went and digged in the earth, and hid his lord's money. After a long time the lord of those servants cometh, and reckoneth with them. And so he that had received five talents came and brought other five talents, saying, Lord, thou deliveredst unto me five talents: behold, I have gained beside them five talents more. His lord said unto him, Well done, thou good and faithful servant: thou hast been faithful over a few things, I will make thee ruler over many things: enter thou into the joy of thy lord. He also that had received two talents came and said, Lord, thou deliveredst unto me two talents: behold, I have gained two other talents beside them. His lord said unto him, Well done, good and faithful

servant; thou hast been faithful over a few things, I will make thee ruler over many things: enter thou into the joy of thy lord. Then he which had received the one talent came and said, Lord, I knew thee that thou art an hard man, reaping where thou hast not sown, and gathering where thou hast not strawed: And I was afraid, and went and hid thy talent in the earth: lo, there thou hast that is thine. His lord answered and said unto him, Thou wicked and slothful servant, thou knewest that I reap where I sowed not, and gather where I have not strawed: Thou oughtest therefore to have put my money to the exchangers, and then at my coming I should have received mine own with usury. Take therefore the talent from him, and give it unto him which hath ten talents. For unto every one that hath shall be given, and he shall have abundance: but from him that hath not shall be taken away even that which he hath. And cast ye the unprofitable servant into outer darkness: there shall be weeping and gnashing of teeth." Matthew 25:14-30.

Only what is done for Christ will last. Are you valuing the little bit He has given you to use for His service?

Do you consider your own worldly valuables more important than serving God? Jesus came across a young man who thought he wanted to follow Jesus until the light was shone on what he considered valuable.

"Then Jesus beholding him loved him, and said unto him, One thing thou lackest: go thy way, sell whatsoever thou hast, and give to the poor, and thou shalt have treasure in heaven: and come, take up the cross, and follow me. And he was sad at that saying, and went away grieved: for he had great possessions." Mark 10:21-22.

We let position, prestige, possessions, popularity, and personality become more valuable and treasured than what God considers to be treasure.

Treasures in Darkness

Throughout this treasure hunt, there have been many dark times. It seemed as if escape into the light would never happen. Too often, I did not value the darkness that was surrounding me, or at least the feelings that the darkness invoked. As I read my personal devotions this morning, a phrase leaped out at me about treasures in darkness. What could possibly be so wonderful about darkness?

Psalm 112:1-4 gave me a glimpse of this possibility of treasure in darkness.

"Praise ye the LORD. Blessed is the man that feareth the LORD, that delighteth greatly in his commandments. His seed shall be mighty upon earth: the generation of the upright shall be blessed. Wealth and riches shall be in his house: and his righteousness endureth for ever. Unto the upright there ariseth light in the darkness: he is gracious, and full of compassion, and righteous."

When we let Jesus into our darkness, He is the light, the lamp, the way out of our darkness. There is, however, a purpose for some of the dark times in our lives. Tribulation works to strengthen our faith, to make us as strong as diamonds, and rich in mercy and grace. When you are going through dark days, you are searching for a light, a rescue, an escape… will you let Jesus be all that for you? This verse in 1 Kings reminds me that God is in my darkness. *"Then spake Solomon, The LORD said that he would dwell in the thick darkness."* 1 Kings 8:12.

Another amazing example of the treasure in darkness comes from the life of Esther. She trusted God without evidence or signs of help or hope. Yet, look at the immeasurable gains of her dark trial of faith. We could say the same for Job, Joseph, Noah, and so many other faithful witnesses of the treasures in darkness.

The answer to why we go through dark times might be something that we have stated before, that the trying of our faith worketh patience.

Let's look at this jewel in James. *"My brethren, count it all joy when ye fall into divers temptations; Knowing this, that the trying of your faith worketh patience. But let patience have her perfect work, that ye may be perfect and entire, wanting nothing. If any of you lack wisdom, let him ask of God, that giveth to all men liberally, and upbraideth not; and it shall be given him."* James 1:2-5.

Patience is not a gem that we collect very much of in our treasure chest, here is another jewel in James. *"Behold, we count them happy which endure. Ye have heard of the patience of Job, and have seen the end of the Lord; that the Lord is very pitiful, and of tender mercy."* James 5:11.

Reading through a devotional written in the last century, it states that patience takes away worry, weakness, and wobbling. Patience leads to worship! That, my friends, is a treasure, a gem worth discovering! Tribulation brings transformation and thus treasure!

When you study how gems are made naturally in the darkness of the earth you will understand how applicable a comparison this is for our study of the treasure of darkness. Did you know that gold is mentioned over four hundred times in Scripture? It's held in high regard for its value, purity, and resilience. Did you catch that last word? Resilience? Just because these are dark days, and life is hard does not mean that God is not at work carving facets in our faith, shining a golden light on our journey, or guiding us through the pits of despair. We have talked repeatedly in these devotional entries about tribulation and patience, but what about hope and help? Researching how many times darkness of any sort is mentioned in the Bible, it shows up about 175 times in varying forms, but light is used over two hundred times! As one person so aptly described it, light is a major golden thread that runs through the Bible!

We have heard the phrase there is a silver lining in every cloud. Did you know that silver is mentioned over three hundred times in the Bible? That silver lining refers to hope!

What are your favorite treasured verses about hope?

_____

_____

How many verses can you find about God being our help?

_____

_____

"That the trial of your faith, being much more precious than of gold that perisheth, though it be tried with fire, might be found unto praise and honour and glory at the appearing of Jesus Christ: Whom having not seen, ye love; in whom, though now ye see him not, yet believing, ye rejoice with joy unspeakable and full of glory: Receiving the end of your faith, even the salvation of your souls." 1 Peter 1:7-9

Treasure of Light

"Then shall the righteous shine forth as the sun in the kingdom of their Father. Who hath ears to hear, let him hear." Matthew 13:43.

Where does this treasure of light come from? John's Gospel tells us *"In the beginning was the Word, and the Word was with God, and the Word was God. The same was in the beginning with God. All things were made by him; and without him was not any thing made that was made. In him was life; and the life was the light of men. And the light shineth in darkness; and the darkness comprehended it not."* John 1:1-5.

Jesus is the Light of the world; we as His children reflect that light and shall shine forth as the sun, or we could also say as the Son! How do we keep our lights shining? *"Ye are the light of the world. A city that is set on an hill cannot be hid. Neither do men light a candle, and put it under a bushel, but on a candlestick; and it giveth light unto all that are in the house. Let your light so shine before men, that they may see your good works, and glorify your Father which is in heaven."* Matthew 5:14-16.

Maybe as you grew up you heard this little chorus, "This little light of mine, I'm gonna let it shine…" Was this song only for children? There are many things that will try to hide or blow out this light that we carry within us. However, in searching for treasures associated with light, I came across a verse in Romans that completely took me by surprise. *"The night is far spent, the day is at hand: let us therefore cast off the works of darkness, and let us put on the armour of light."* Romans 13:12. In Ephesians, you are probably aware of the armor of God listed piece by piece in chapter six starting with verse ten.

"Finally, my brethren, be strong in the Lord, and in the power of his might. Put on the whole armour of God, that ye may

be able to stand against the wiles of the devil. For we wrestle not against flesh and blood, but against principalities, against powers, against the rulers of the darkness of this world, against spiritual wickedness in high places. Wherefore take unto you the whole armour of God, that ye may be able to withstand in the evil day, and having done all, to stand. Stand therefore, having your loins girt about with truth, and having on the breastplate of righteousness; And your feet shod with the preparation of the gospel of peace; Above all, taking the shield of faith, wherewith ye shall be able to quench all the fiery darts of the wicked. And take the helmet of salvation, and the sword of the Spirit, which is the word of God: Praying always with all prayer and supplication in the Spirit, and watching thereunto with all perseverance and supplication for all saints;" Ephesians 6:10-18.

In 2 Corinthians 6:7, it is called the armor of righteousness. The connection to light had gone unnoticed, until now. We have the light, we are to reflect His light, and we are to protect that light with His armor of light. It all goes together, and yet we let angry moods or our dark thoughts shade that light from shining forth. *"Every good gift and every perfect gift is from above, and cometh down from the Father of lights, with whom is no variableness, neither shadow of turning."* James 1:17

Shine the light of God on your life today, and you will find the real treasure that you have been seeking all along.

This little light of mine, I must let it shine, I won't let my angry mood hide it, or let my mind blow it out. This little light of mine must shine all over my little house, town, and world until Jesus comes.

Will you be His treasure of light?

Evil Treasure

How sinister sounding is this? You would think it was straight from the plot of a fairy tale that we read with goosebumps as children. Let me present to you the case of the evil treasure.

James 5:3, *"Your gold and silver is cankered; and the rust of them shall be a witness against you, and shall eat your flesh as it were fire. Ye have heaped treasure together for the last days."*

Picture that! When what you treasure is of this world, it will be a witness against you and only bring evil and not good.

"Therefore mine heart shall sound for Moab like pipes, and mine heart shall sound like pipes for the men of Kirheres: because the riches that he hath gotten are perished." That was found in Jeremiah 48:36. And now look at verse seven, as well. *"For because thou hast trusted in thy works and in thy treasures,thou shalt also be taken:"*

"Or despisest thou the riches of his goodness and forbearance and longsuffering; not knowing that the goodness of God leadeth thee to repentance? But after thy hardness and impenitent heart treasurest up unto thyself wrath against the day of wrath and revelation of the righteous judgment of God; Who will render to every man according to his deeds: To them who by patient continuance in well doing seek for glory and honour and immortality, eternal life: But unto them that are contentious, and do not obey the truth, but obey unrighteousness, indignation and wrath, Tribulation and anguish, upon every soul of man that doeth evil, of the Jew first, and also of the Gentile; But glory, honour, and peace, to every man that worketh good, to the Jew first, and also to the Gentile: For there is no respect of persons with God." Romans 2:4-11.

"Wherefore gloriest thou in the valleys, thy flowing valley, O backsliding daughter? that trusted in her treasures, saying, Who shall come unto me?" Jeremiah 49:4.

"A sword is upon their horses, and upon their chariots, and upon all the mingled people that are in the midst of her; and they shall become as women: a sword is upon her treasures; and they shall be robbed." Jeremiah 50:37.

"O thou that dwellest upon many waters, abundant in treasures, thine end is come, and the measure of thy covetousness." Jeremiah 51:13.

Just in a couple chapters we are reminded over and over again that what we value will reflect where our treasure is. Decide what value earthly wealth has to you over spiritual treasures.

"They that trust in their wealth, and boast themselves in the multitude of their riches; None of them can by any means redeem his brother, nor give to God a ransom for him: (For the redemption of their soul is precious, and it ceaseth for ever:)" Psalms 49:6-8.

Take some time today to read this whole chapter of Psalm 49 to fully grasp what it is saying.

In this space, write out what you have decided has more value: _____

_____

_____

"A good man out of the good treasure of the heart bringeth forth good things: and an evil man out of the evil treasure bringeth forth evil things." Matthew 12:35.

You would not want evil cursed treasure near you, yet that is exactly what you have when you store up evil in your heart and collect earthly treasure out of greed and pride.

"Charge them that are rich in this world, that they be not highminded, nor trust in uncertain riches, but in the living God, who giveth us richly all things to enjoy; That they do good, that

they be rich in good works, ready to distribute, willing to communicate; Laying up in store for themselves a good foundation against the time to come, that they may lay hold on eternal life." 1 Timothy 6:17-19.

Real Gold!

Back when gold was used as currency, it was often easy to mistake pyrite for the real thing. However, fool's gold can flake, powder, or crumble, but real gold will only leave a mark. If you use a piece of gold to scratch something, it will leave a yellow streak. That is the mark that it's real and not fake. History books often tell us how the miners and the merchants would bite down on the proffered currency to test it for authenticity.

"O taste and see that the LORD is good: blessed is the man that trusteth in him." Psalms 34:8, and repeatedly in the book of Psalms we see how the Lord and His Word is compared to treasure.

"I have rejoiced in the way of thy testimonies, as much as in all riches." Psalms 119:14.

"The law of the LORD is perfect, converting the soul: the testimony of the LORD is sure, making wise the simple. The statutes of the LORD are right, rejoicing the heart: the commandment of the LORD is pure, enlightening the eyes. The fear of the LORD is clean, enduring for ever: the judgments of the LORD are true and righteous altogether. More to be desired are they than gold, yea, than much fine gold: sweeter also than honey and the honeycomb. Moreover by them is thy servant warned: and in keeping of them there is great reward." Psalms 19:7-11.

I am sure that the taste of gold left an aftertaste in one's mouth compared to other stones. There is no mention of the taste of gold, and yet, if your teeth left a mark, it was fairly certain that it was real gold. Do you taste-test the Word of God and His treasures for yourself? The Psalmist called them sweet as honey and more to be desired than gold.

"Behold, I will send my messenger, and he shall prepare the way before me: and the Lord, whom ye seek, shall suddenly

come to his temple, even the messenger of the covenant, whom ye delight in: behold, he shall come, saith the LORD of hosts. But who may abide the day of his coming? and who shall stand when he appeareth? for he is like a refiner's fire, and like fullers' soap: And he shall sit as a refiner and purifier of silver: and he shall purify the sons of Levi, and purge them as gold and silver, that they may offer unto the LORD an offering in righteousness." Malachi 3:1-3.

We need to make sure that what we believe is real and authentic, but it also matters what we say and do, for God will try us with His refiner's fire. God is real and does not change, but are you the real thing? When people test you, do you leave a pure golden mark and a soft, rich taste of Heaven in their lives?

Royal Diadem

A beautiful hymn, "All Hail the Power of Jesus Name," has this phrase in it: "Bring forth the royal diadem and crown Him Lord of all." Another hymn is titled "Crown Him with Many Crowns." The word diadem is a type of crown specifically worn by monarchs as a badge of royalty. When we read Revelation, we see that we will crown Jesus as King of kings and Lord of lords. What are these crowns that we will crown Him with?

First of all, these crowns will be incorruptible, not earthly or man-made. 1 Corinthians 9:25, *"And every man that striveth for the mastery is temperate in all things. Now they do it to obtain a corruptible crown; but we an incorruptible."*

Let's look at some of these incorruptible crowns that we will have the glorious privilege and honor to humbly give to our Savior, King Jesus. 1 Thessalonians 2:19 speaks of a crown of rejoicing, *"For what is our hope, or joy, or crown of rejoicing?"* Study this chapter to get the context, but if we would consider rejoicing as a crown to give to the Lord, might we not do more rejoicing and less complaining?

2 Timothy 4:8 names another crown. *"Henceforth there is laid up for me a crown of righteousness, which the Lord, the righteous judge, shall give me at that day: and not to me only, but unto all them also that love his appearing."* What is righteousness? Putting it simply, it means living right. We know what is right only if we read and obey the Scripture as it defines what is right. This is just a simple explanation, yet we find it so hard to live right. Were we to remember that we get a crown to give the Lord for doing and living right, would we not be more inclined to live a holy, godly life?

James 1:12 names another crown: *"Blessed is the man that endureth temptation: for when he is tried, he shall receive the crown of life, which the Lord hath promised to them that love him."*

"And the LORD their God shall save them in that day as the flock of his people: for they shall be as the stones of a crown, lifted up as an ensign upon his land." Zechariah 9:16.

Let's recap for a minute. A crown of rejoicing, a crown of righteousness, and now a crown of life. When we look at those, it simply means that with the joy of the Lord as your strength, you can live right and endure temptation. Live a life that shows that you love the Lord no matter what situation you are in.

These crowns are given to those citizens of Heaven in service to the King, the faithful stewards who answer the Great Commission and cultivate lives of spiritual treasure.

Are there any other crowns? Look at 1 Peter 5:4, what crown do you see in this verse?

Bring forth the royal diadem; it's coronation time! *"And when those beasts give glory and honour and thanks to him that sat on the throne, who liveth for ever and ever, The four and twenty elders fall down before him that sat on the throne, and worship him that liveth for ever and ever, and cast their crowns before the throne, saying, Thou art worthy, O Lord, to receive glory and honour and power: for thou hast created all things, and for thy pleasure they are and were created."* Revelation 4:9-11.

"His eyes were as a flame of fire, and on his head were many crowns; and he had a name written, that no man knew, but he himself. And he was clothed with a vesture dipped in blood: and his name is called The Word of God. And the armies which were in heaven followed him upon white horses, clothed in fine linen, white and clean. And out of his mouth goeth a sharp sword, that with it he should smite the nations: and he shall rule them with a rod of iron: and he treadeth the winepress of the

fierceness and wrath of Almighty God. And he hath on his vesture and on his thigh a name written, KING OF KINGS, AND LORD OF LORDS. " Revelation 19:12-16.

Is Jesus your King? Will He receive back any crowns from the life you lived that illustrates that He is your Sovereign, your Authority?

Great Treasure

"Receive my instruction, and not silver; and knowledge rather than choice gold. For wisdom is better than rubies; and all the things that may be desired are not to be compared to it." Proverbs 8:10-11.

"I wisdom dwell with prudence, and find out knowledge of witty inventions. The fear of the LORD is to hate evil: pride, and arrogancy, and the evil way, and the froward mouth, do I hate. Counsel is mine, and sound wisdom: I am understanding; I have strength. By me kings reign, and princes decree justice. By me princes rule and nobles, even all the judges of the earth. I love them that love me; and those that seek me early shall find me. Riches and honour are with me; yea, durable riches and righteousness. My fruit is better than gold, yea, than fine gold; and my revenue than choice silver. I lead in the way of righteousness, in the midst of the paths of judgment: That I may cause those that love me to inherit substance; and I will fill their treasures." Proverbs 8:12-21.

As you read that passage did you catch the treasure in there? Wisdom is great treasure! Not wordly, sinful knowledge and arrogance, but wisdom from God. In other devotionals, we touch upon the treasures of wisdom. However, it is necessary to continue to search for it and to store it up in our hearts and lives. Having true wisdom is better than having all the wealth of the world.

The book of Proverbs is all about wisdom and its true meaning and purpose. Too many of us would rather be fools as this book also warns adamantly against.

"By humility and the fear of the LORD are riches, and honour, and life." Proverbs 22:4.

Let's go to the book about wisdom found in the New Testament – James.

"If any of you lack wisdom, let him ask of God, that giveth to all men liberally, and upbraideth not; and it shall be given him. But let him ask in faith, nothing wavering. For he that wavereth is like a wave of the sea driven with the wind and tossed. For let not that man think that he shall receive any thing of the Lord. A double minded man is unstable in all his ways. Let the brother of low degree rejoice in that he is exalted: But the rich, in that he is made low: because as the flower of the grass he shall pass away. For the sun is no sooner risen with a burning heat, but it withereth the grass, and the flower thereof falleth, and the grace of the fashion of it perisheth: so also shall the rich man fade away in his ways." James 1:5-11.

All throughout the treasure of God's rich, inerrant Word, He is threading wisdom throughout as a weaver would using threads of gold to bring more value to the finished work. Will you let this great treasure be woven into the very tapestry of your life? Did you know that the word wisdom is mentioned over 222 times in the Word of God? A secular search of this states that wisdom was regarded as one of the highest virtues along with kindness. That is from a secular source! Stop for a minute and think about that! We know that the primary writer of Proverbs was Solomon, who asked God for wisdom. This prayerful request was answered in divine abundance and earthly riches untold were also given. Yet, again, Solomon writes *"How much better is it to get wisdom than gold! and to get understanding rather to be chosen than silver!"* Proverbs 16:16.

Do you want to have great treasure? *"Get wisdom, get understanding: forget it not; neither decline from the words of my mouth. Forsake her not, and she shall preserve thee: love her, and she shall keep thee. Wisdom is the principal thing; therefore get wisdom: and with all thy getting get understanding. Exalt her, and she shall promote thee: she shall bring thee to honour, when thou dost embrace her. She shall give to thine head an ornament of grace: a crown of glory shall she deliver to thee.*" Proverbs 4:5-9.

"*But the wisdom that is from above is first pure, then peaceable, gentle, and easy to be intreated, full of mercy and good fruits, without partiality, and without hypocrisy.*" James 3:17.

Discovered Treasure

Eureka! I found it! When you discover treasure, there is usually a burst of verbal exaltation, even if you are sneaking around in hopes that no one else will notice what you are doing. There is just something that wells up within us when we find something worth having. Treasure hunting takes time, hard work, effort, patience, wisdom, knowledge, protection, alertness, and the list goes on. Yet we do not even want to make a smidgen of an effort when it comes to hunting spiritual treasure.

When you find a nugget in the Word of God, does it cause you to well up inside and burst out with verbal recognition that you have found gold? As we search through Scripture, do we uncover truth, those jewels of everlasting value?

How do you react when God does wondrous things in your life and in your church?

"And when the builders laid the foundation of the temple of the LORD, they set the priests in their apparel with trumpets, and the Levites the sons of Asaph with cymbals, to praise the LORD, after the ordinance of David king of Israel. And they sang together by course in praising and giving thanks unto the LORD; because he is good, for his mercy endureth for ever toward Israel. And all the people shouted with a great shout, when they praised the LORD, because the foundation of the house of the LORD was laid. But many of the priests and Levites and chief of the fathers, who were ancient men, that had seen the first house, when the foundation of this house was laid before their eyes, wept with a loud voice; and many shouted aloud for joy: So that the people could not discern the noise of the shout of joy from the noise of the weeping of the people: for the people shouted with a loud shout, and the noise was heard afar off." Ezra 3:10-13.

Repeatedly through Scripture, we are told to shout, sing, rejoice, and to lift up our voice to proclaim His praise. Have you discovered, uncovered this hidden treasure of worship? We have often fallen into the mindset that holiness means solemn silence. We think intoned benedictions and ritualistic motions are the formula for praising God. When we discover treasure, it's a subconscious almost natural reaction to verbally exclaim! Why is it then, that we think praising the King of kings should be hushed and sanctimonious?

Discover the great treasure of shouting praises to the Lord! For He is worthy!

"And after these things I heard a great voice of much people in heaven, saying, Alleluia; Salvation, and glory, and honour, and power, unto the Lord our God: For true and righteous are his judgments: for he hath judged the great whore, which did corrupt the earth with her fornication, and hath avenged the blood of his servants at her hand. And again they said, Alleluia. And her smoke rose up for ever and ever. And the four and twenty elders and the four beasts fell down and worshipped God that sat on the throne, saying, Amen; Alleluia. And a voice came out of the throne, saying, Praise our God, all ye his servants, and ye that fear him, both small and great. And I heard as it were the voice of a great multitude, and as the voice of many waters, and as th e voice of mighty thunderings, saying, Alleluia: for the Lord God omnipotent reigneth. Let us be glad and rejoice, and give honour to him: for the marriage of the Lamb is come, and his wife hath made herself ready. And to her was granted that she should be arrayed in fine linen, clean and white: for the fine linen is the righteousness of saints." Revelation 19:1-8.

On your own treasure hunt today, look up the Scripture in Revelation that states, "Worthy is the Lamb:_____
_____
"

Did you discover great treasure in that passage?

Borrowed Treasures

A well-known Southern gospel song has a phrase in it that opines the things that we love and hold dear are not ours they are just borrowed. What borrowed treasures do we have?

Our life is a borrowed treasure from the Giver of life. Do we treat our lives as treasure?

"Go to now, ye that say, To day or to morrow we will go into such a city, and continue there a year, and buy and sell, and get gain: Whereas ye know not what shall be on the morrow. For what is your life? It is even a vapour, that appeareth for a little time, and then vanisheth away." James 4:13-14.

Our children are borrowed treasures: *"Lo, children are an heritage of the LORD: and the fruit of the womb is his reward."* Psalms 127:3.

Talent, skills, and abilities are treasures given by God to be used for His glory. Interestingly, the word talent in Bible times was a measurement of weight, a currency value. Our word today is defined as a mental or physical strength that can be useful in pursuit of art or a profession. The word went from denoting value by weight, to denoting value by what we are skilled at doing. What has God given you the ability to do well that can be used for an eternal weight in Glory?

Look up 1 Corinthians 10:31 and write it here:

_____

_____

_____

Our time, our talents, and our children are all borrowed treasures. Our life here on earth is only enriched by knowing that we are just stewards, keeping the King's treasures safely and profitably until He returns to collect them.

Peace of Eight

Pirates are notoriously famous for using pieces of eight. This was a Spanish dollar coin that could literally be split into pieces. For our treasure hunt today, let's play on the phrase and see if we can find value in the peace of eight. After a light search, it was suggested that there are eight principles of peace: faith, God's Word, compassion, gratitude, prayer, forgiveness, repentance, and hope. While searching on this topic, I noticed that too many times not all eight of these are mentioned. Some internet sites talk about five keys to peace, or three or four, but not eight.

Then, I did a query about people in the Bible that might be called people of peace. One website mentioned these as people who welcomed the Word of God. The Centurion in Luke 7, the Samaritan Woman in John 4, the Ethiopian Eunuch in Acts 8, Cornelius in Acts 10, Lydia in Acts 16, and the Philippian jailer in Acts 16. These are the first six, so can you think of at least two more?

_____

_____

(Try 1 Corinthians 16:19)

As I was searching on my own treasure hunt, I noticed how the Apostle Paul ended most of his epistles with words of peace.

2 Corinthians 13:11, *"Finally, brethren, farewell. Be perfect, be of good comfort, be of one mind, live in peace; and the God of love and peace shall be with you."*

Galatians 6:16, *"And as many as walk according to this rule, peace be on them, and mercy, and upon the Israel of God."*

Ephesians 6 mentions peace as a vital part of the armor of God and then concludes with a salutation of peace in verse twenty-three. Which part of the armor is this?

1 Thessalonians 5:23 is a prayer for peace, which piece of peace does this one line up with?

---

2 Thessalonians 3:16 write this verse out:

_____

_____

Hebrews 13:20-21 What does the God of peace do as outlined in these verses?

Here are just six pieces of peace. This word according to my research is used over 429 times in the Bible, and yet rarely do we seem to have peace. The peace that passeth all understanding only comes from God. If you want to have the peace of God, you have to be at peace with God. Again, it seems we do not have all eight pieces. Can you find two more verses about peace in the Bible?

When peace like a river attendeth my way… "It Is Well With My Soul," a song most treasured in my life, speaks of having peace in the middle of the hardest tragedies. Peace, peace, wonderful peace, coming down from the Father above… Many of our hymns and spiritual songs speak of peace, and yet, like Scripture says, too many times, we cry for peace, and we have none.

At the beginning of today's treasure hunt, we talked about different principles of peace. These verses in Colossians seem to summarize those principles of peace. _"Put on therefore, as the elect of God, holy and beloved, bowels of mercies, kindness, humbleness of mind, meekness, longsuffering; Forbearing one another, and forgiving one another, if any man_ *have a quarrel against any: even as Christ forgave you, so also do ye. And above all these things put on charity, which is the bond of perfectness. And let the peace of God rule in your hearts, to the which also ye are called in one body; and be ye thankful. Let the word of Christ dwell in you richly in all wisdom; teaching and admonishing one another in psalms and hymns and spiritual songs, singing with grace in your hearts to the Lord. And whatsoever ye do in word or deed, do all in the name of the Lord Jesus, giving thanks to God and the Father by him."* Colossians 3:12-17

Our peace of eight has been eight principles of peace, eight people of peace, and eight passages of Scripture about peace. How many pieces of peace do you have?

Treasured Thoughts

"And thou, Solomon my son, know thou the God of thy father, and serve him with a perfect heart and with a willing mind: for the LORD searcheth all hearts, and understandeth all the imaginations of the thoughts: if thou seek him, he will be found of thee; but if thou forsake him, he will cast thee off for ever." 1 Chronicles 28:9.

"I know also, my God, that thou triest the heart, and hast pleasure in uprightness. As for me, in the uprightness of mine heart I have willingly offered all these things: and now have I seen with joy thy people, which are present here, to offer willingly unto thee. O LORD God of Abraham, Isaac, and of Israel, our fathers, keep this for ever in the imagination of the thoughts of the heart of thy people, and prepare their heart unto thee:" 1 Chronicles 29:17-18.

What are you thinking about? Are your thoughts and imaginations evil continually or upright and centered on God?

"The wicked, through the pride of his countenance, will not seek after God: God is not in all his thoughts." Psalms 10:4.

Do you treasure what God thinks? We may not know all that is in the mind of God, but we do know through Scripture what thoughts He treasures.

"The counsel of the LORD standeth for ever, the thoughts of his heart to all generations." Psalms 33:11.

"Many, O LORD my God, are thy wonderful works which thou hast done, and thy thoughts which are to us-ward: they cannot be reckoned up in order unto thee: if I would declare and speak of them, they are more than can be numbered." Psalms 40:5.

God's thoughts are upon us. His ways may not be our ways, but He is always thinking about us!

Personally, with fear and trembling that is a great treasure to me.

"For my thoughts are not your thoughts, neither are your ways my ways, saith the LORD. For as the heavens are higher than the earth, so are my ways higher than your ways, and my thoughts than your thoughts." Isaiah 55:8-9.

"For I know the thoughts that I think toward you, saith the LORD, thoughts of peace, and not of evil, to give you an expected end. Then shall ye call upon me, and ye shall go and pray unto me, and I will hearken unto you. And ye shall seek me, and find me, when ye shall search for me with all your heart." Jeremiah 29:11-14.

Look up Proverbs 12:5 and write down what it says about thoughts: _____

_____

Now look up Proverbs 15:26, 16:3, and 21:5 and compare these verses to see what type of thoughts we should treasure.

Repeatedly throughout Scripture, we are told what sort of thoughts to treasure, what thoughts will honor and glorify God.

In the next few devotional entries, we will specifically break down different thoughts to treasure based on Philippians 4:8.

True Treasure

"Finally, brethren, whatsoever things are true, whatsoever things are honest, whatsoever things are just, whatsoever things are pure, whatsoever things are lovely, whatsoever things are of good report; if there be any virtue, and if there be any praise, think on these things. Those things, which ye have both learned, and received, and heard, and seen in me, do: and the God of peace shall be with you." Philippians 4:8-9.

The first thought to treasure is listed as "True." Puzzling over this, the Lord showed me that by thinking only of things that are true will we be truly content. When we bring our thoughts into the obedience of Christ, the truth of God brings peace and satisfaction. Too often, our minds are blinded or seduced by the world, our flesh, or the deception of the devil.

How do we know what is true? The Word of God is true, as we see in John 1:14. *"And the Word was made flesh, and dwelt among us, (and we beheld his glory, the glory as of the only begotten of the Father,) full of grace and truth."* However, it's not just the Word, He IS the Word!

Jesus repeats this truth about Himself in John 14:6, *"Jesus saith unto him, I am the way, the truth, and the life: no man cometh unto the Father, but by me."*

When you think about Jesus and who He is and what He says, when you follow His way, you will be thinking thoughts that are true, for He is truth.

The armor of God even hinges on truth! Look at Ephesians 6, *"Wherefore take unto you the whole armour of God, that ye may be able to withstand in the evil day, and having done all, to stand. Stand therefore, having your loins girt about with truth, and having on the breastplate of righteousness; And your feet shod with the preparation of the gospel of peace; Above all, taking the shield of faith, wherewith ye shall be able to quench all the fiery darts of the wicked. And take the helmet of salvation, and the sword of the Spirit, which is the word of God: Praying always with all prayer and supplication in the Spirit, and watching thereunto with all perseverance and supplication for all saints;"* Ephesians 6:13-18.

"But if I tarry long, that thou mayest know how thou oughtest to behave thyself in the house of God, which is the church of the living God, the pillar and ground of the truth." 1 Timothy 3:15.

Did you catch that? Pull yourself together and center yourself with truth because every tool that you will need to use to fight and stand in this spiritual battle is going to be based on truth. Truth being the very thing that holds and keeps you together. How effective you are in this battle depends on how much you think on things that are true!

So, Jesus is Truth, and His Word is truth, and His church is truth!

"And I saw heaven opened, and behold a white horse; and he that sat upon him was called Faithful and True, and in righteousness he doth judge and make war. His eyes were as a flame of fire, and on his head were many crowns; and he had a name written, that no man knew, but he himself. And he was clothed with a vesture dipped in blood: and his name is called The Word of God. And the armies which were in heaven followed him upon white horses, clothed in fine linen, white and clean. And out of his mouth goeth a sharp sword, that with it he should smite the nations: and he shall rule them with a rod of iron: and he treadeth the winepress of the fierceness and wrath of Almighty God. And he hath on his vesture and on his thigh a name written, KING OF KINGS, AND LORD OF LORDS." Revelation 19:11-16.

Think on these things!

Mining Integrity

As we continue with Philippians 4:8, the second thing that we are supposed to think on is honesty. Now, wait, doesn't that mean the same thing as truth? Why the delineation between the two words? Let's consider that if we think about things that are true, then we will henceforth do those true things, which will lead us to lead honest lives.

When I looked up the definition of honest, I was struck by how many times the word integrity was used. How you think is how you live... You are what you think is very succinct! No wonder this verse in Philippians 4:8 tells us what we need to be thinking about.

Where can we find integrity? We need to mine for it! Let's go mining for integrity in Scripture.

"And if thou wilt walk before me, as David thy father walked, in integrity of heart, and in uprightness, to do according to all that I have commanded thee, and wilt keep my statutes and my judgments:" 1 Kings 9:4.

What a precious jewel to be found, if you finish reading the context, you'll see that the promise of God hinges on walking in the integrity of heart and uprightness. This is the very definition of truth in action.

Finding someone who has integrity and uprightness is actually rare. It's much easier to find someone who is not trustworthy, who seems to thrive on deceit and falsehood. If things that are TRUE are the mine, then things that are honest is the ore to be mined. In our case it needs to be in our minds and hearts!

"Let integrity and uprightness preserve me; for I wait on thee." Psalms 25:21.

"Judge me, O LORD; for I have walked in mine integrity: I have trusted also in the LORD; therefore I shall not

slide. Examine me, O LORD, and prove me; try my reins and my heart. For thy lovingkindness is before mine eyes: and I have walked in thy truth." Psalms 26:1-3.

Can you say the same thing to the Lord? Are you mining integrity? Those who are full of integrity can be trusted which in itself is a real treasure.

Now, the actual word in Philippians 4:8 was honest. It was defined as integrity by the dictionary. We mined a few verses about integrity, however, there is much more still to be mined.

What verses do you find about being honest? Besides our main text, a quick search showed me five verses that use the word "honest." Interestingly enough, they really seemed to echo our core verse in Philippians 4:8.

Which ones have you unearthed?

_____

_____

_____

_____

Getting to the Core

We have mined for integrity; we have treasured what is true, but the core here, the middle of the mine is the word "just." Again, it seems to be related to truth, honesty, and integrity, so why would it be separated and delineated for us to think on?

Looking up the meaning of the word in a secular dictionary, it talks about what is fair and righteous. Now, for a secular dictionary to use the word righteous ought to get your attention.

What is righteous? Living right, but what is the right way to live? If your life and your thoughts are not centered on the righteousness of God, then your own righteousness is clearly just filthy rags. Scripture says that men are known to do that which is right in their own eyes. Not only are we to have thoughts based on the truth of God, to live in integrity based on His standards, but we are also to be fair and righteous in all our ways.

Let's look at what God says about being just. *"Judges and officers shalt thou make thee in all thy gates, which the LORD thy God giveth thee, throughout thy tribes: and they shall judge the people with just judgment. Thou shalt not wrest judgment; thou shalt not respect persons, neither take a gift: for a gift doth blind the eyes of the wise, and pervert the words of the righteous. That which is altogether just shalt thou follow, that thou mayest live, and inherit the land which the LORD thy God giveth thee."* Deuteronomy 16:18-20.

His command was for His people to be just and to deal justly in all their decisions. When you think about how you handle things, the storms and problems in life, do you think about how fair and just it is? Not usually, too many times we hear about how unfair we have it. Are you treating others with the same fairness that you want to be treated with?

"Because I will publish the name of the LORD: ascribe ye greatness unto our God. He is the Rock, his work is perfect: for all his ways are judgment: a God of truth and without iniquity, just and right is he." Deuteronomy 32:3-4.

"But the path of the just is as the shining light, that shineth more and more unto the perfect day." Proverbs 4:18.

Not only are we to think on things that are just, but we will find that our path through this evil world will be shining brightly in front of us as we walk in His truth, His integrity, His uprightness, His definition of what is right and just!

Think on this!

Pure Gold

Are your thoughts pure, without spot or blemish? Or are you under the control of stinkin' thinkin'? We could just get stuck in looking at all the verses on the use of pure gold. However, this study is more about what is pure in our hearts and minds.

The Bible is rich in the abundance of verses about pure and purity. Let's dig into a few while we are right here in this gold mine.

"Who shall ascend into the hill of the LORD? or who shall stand in his holy place? He that hath clean hands, and a pure heart; who hath not lifted up his soul unto vanity, nor sworn deceitfully. He shall receive the blessing from the LORD, and righteousness from the God of his salvation." Psalms 24:3-5.

Did you grab onto that treasure? Clean hands, not guilty of murder or injustice, not vain, not a liar, but one who is pure in heart will be able to enter into the Kingdom of the LORD.

"The thoughts of the wicked are an abomination to the LORD: but the words of the pure are pleasant words." Proverbs 15:26.

When we look at the next thought to treasure, come back to this verse in Proverbs and see how it describes not just the pure but the lovely! What you think will indeed come out of your mouth! That is why it's so important to have pure thoughts. Here again Scripture expands on the thought, *"Who can say, I have made my heart clean, I am pure from my sin? Divers weights, and divers measures, both of them are alike abomination to the LORD. Even a child is known by his doings, whether his work be pure, and whether it be right. The hearing ear, and the seeing eye, the LORD hath made even both of them."* Proverbs 20:9-12.

What is in your heart will come out your mouth, in what you do, what you listen to, and what you watch.

This is just a snapshot, a glimpse of the pearl of purity, the treasure of pure gold that we are to be putting to use in our thought life.

Oh! That's Lovely!

Here we are in the middle of a treasure hunt for the eight pieces of treasured thoughts. We just hit the core of the mine, and voila` what did we find - just the most lovely of all jewels!

This jewel is so lovely that we are not even sure what to think about it, much less describe it. Definitions like acceptable and pleasing just don't seem to do it justice. Are you noticing all the play on words of the things we are already to be treasuring in our thoughts?

This jewel should be so valuable and dear to the heart of man because it reveals the treasure that is held within our heart. This jewel called LOVELY displays what or Who we worship. Worship – to give honor and glory to, to proclaim worth!

Sadly, too many times, we taint this word with sarcasm; we tarnish its true meaning with falsehood. Are your thoughts centered upon lovely things? This needs to go deeper than buttercups and daisies. Do your thoughts inspire love and affection?

Our verse in Philippians 4:8 says, *"Whatsoever things are lovely,"* is what we need to be thinking about. Lovely, what does that bring to your mind? When I searched for Scripture using this word, I found that it described people or music.

The people and music were pleasant and beautiful, so then I turned my search to well pleased. The majority of Scripture using the phrase "well pleased" was in reference to God's description of Jesus! Jesus is the very picture of what is lovely, Who we are to be thinking about.

Expanding my search parameters, I looked up Scripture for "well-pleasing," and I only found one, in reference to obedience.

When you think of the word "lovely," you would not even think of obedience as a definition. Yet, one of the very reasons that Jesus is considered all that is lovely, is because of His obedience to God the Father!

While searching for the phrase that came to mind, "He is altogether lovely," I found a sermon by Spurgeon that so elegantly expounds on this verse found in Song of Solomon 5:16. His description was full of words of gold and silver, yet nothing can compare in loveliness to our Lord.

"His mouth is most sweet: yea, he is altogether lovely. This is my beloved, and this is my friend, O daughters of Jerusalem."

When you think upon the Word, and obey what He, the Lovely One has said, you will indeed be able to think on things that are lovely!

Silver Tones

Maybe you have heard the expression silver tongued or silver tones, each of these actually have a different definition. When we speak, are we sounding deceptively sweet, or are our words truly sweet to the ear and heart? Our passage in Philippians 4:8 speaks of thinking upon things of good report.

The secular world thinks this means to be clear, concise, just the facts, no emotion or agenda in reference to the retelling of an incident. Other sources talk about having a good testimony, but what does Scripture say?

It seems simple and concise to me; what you say and do will be spoken about in the manner in which it was received. Do you have a good testimony? Is your speech full of grace seasoned just right with the salt of the Scripture?

"The thoughts of the wicked are an abomination to the LORD: but the words of the pure are pleasant words. He that is greedy of gain troubleth his own house; but he that hateth gifts shall live. The heart of the righteous studieth to answer: but the mouth of the wicked poureth out evil things. The LORD is far from the wicked: but he heareth the prayer of the righteous. The light of the eyes rejoiceth the heart: and a good report maketh the bones fat." Proverbs 15:26-30.

Herein is the difference laid forth for our meditation. We can see similar Scripture about the tongue in the book of James. As I searched out Scripture usage on this phrase "good report" it was more than just what the person said, it was how they lived! Did they have a good testimony or an evil testimony?

When you dig for treasure to think about this, did this passage in Psalms come to your mind?

Think on these things: *"The law of the LORD is perfect, converting the soul: the testimony of the LORD is sure, making wise the simple. The statutes of the LORD are right, rejoicing the heart: the commandment of the LORD is pure, enlightening the eyes. The fear of the LORD is clean, enduring for ever: the judgments of the LORD are true and righteous altogether. More to be desired are they than gold, yea, than much fine gold: sweeter also than honey and the honeycomb. Moreover by them is thy servant warned: and in keeping of them there is great reward. Who can understand his errors? cleanse thou me from secret faults. Keep back thy servant also from presumptuous sins; let them not have dominion over me: then shall I be upright, and I shall be innocent from the great transgression. Let the words of my mouth, and the meditation of my heart, be acceptable in thy sight, O LORD, my strength, and my redeemer."* Psalms 19:7-14.

Virtue Assayed

Our current study has us digging into Philippians 4:8 and studying out each thing that the Apostle Paul tells us to think about. We have reached the mysterious word *"virtue."* "If there be any virtue…" What does *virtue* actually mean?

This multi-faceted word has been defined as the highest moral excellence, virility, bravery, courage, purity, and power.

The word *assay* is defined as determining the quality or content of gold or precious metal. This seemed fitting for this study into virtue. We will assay the quality of our virtue as illustrated in various passages of Scripture.

As we look through Scripture, we find Proverbs 31 illustrating the worth of a virtuous woman. The "-ous" suffix means full of, overflowing. This woman was full of moral excellence, you could say she was full of sacrificial service to others, and courage could define her. *"Who can find a virtuous woman? for her price is far above rubies."* Proverbs 31:10.

However, when we get to the story of the woman with the issue of blood who touched just the hem of Jesus' garment, it's stated that virtue went out from Him. *"And Jesus, immediately knowing in himself that virtue had gone out of him, turned him about in the press, and said, Who touched my clothes?"* Mark 5:30-31.

Let's assay this statement of Christ. Valor, courage, strength, power, masculinity, none of these words seem to describe what transpired. The woman had courage, yet the virtue was not attributed to her. Jesus was sinless, so of course, He was of the highest moral excellence. However, this does not seem to be the meaning of what He felt went out from Him. It did not say strength, or healing, or power. It could have, this woman needed strength and healing, but it used a specific word – *virtue*. This could easily be the definition of virtue that denotes purity, this woman had a disorder that left her unclean. When she touched the hem of His garment, she was made clean and pure!

"And the whole multitude sought to touch him: for there went virtue out of him, and healed them all." Luke 6:19. However, in our Philippians 4:8 passage the word pure is used separately.

We thus see the apostles use this word meaning in their writings, as a call to be holy, godly, and pure in our Christian lives. So, in the story of the woman, purity might be the definition, however, Websters 1828 alludes to this passage by defining it as acting power that has an effect.

Just like gold needs to be assayed, this word is so multi-faceted that you must appreciate every definition that is displayed from its lustrous design. Upon further examination, you find that this word can also be defined as goodness, holiness, along with purity and perfection.

When our key passage said to think about things pertaining to virtue, what does that mean to you?

_____

_____

_____

If your definition and model of virtue were assayed, would it have the same spiritual value as described in Scripture?

"Grace and peace be multiplied unto you through the knowledge of God, and of Jesus our Lord, According as his divine power hath given unto us all things that pertain unto life and godliness, through the knowledge of him that hath called us to glory and virtue:" 2 Peter 1:2-3.

"And beside this, giving all diligence, add to your faith virtue; and to virtue knowledge; And to knowledge temperance; and to temperance patience; and to patience godliness; And to godliness brotherly kindness; and to brotherly kindness charity. For if these things be in you, and abound, they make you that ye

shall neither be barren nor unfruitful in the knowledge of our Lord Jesus Christ." 2 Peter 1:5-8.

Radiant Resonance

Philippians 4:8 has been our recent study of treasures to collect and use. The final thought that we are to think upon is also the seventh in number. Seven is the number of perfection and completion in Scripture. It is no mistake that "Praise" is this final thought to grab onto. Praise, what is this all about?

Our total purpose is to glorify God, to give praise to Him. *"But thou art holy, O thou that inhabitest the praises of Israel. Our fathers trusted in thee: they trusted, and thou didst deliver them."* Psalms 22:3-4. He lives in, actually dwells in the praise of His people. This is better illustrated in Colossians 3:15-17 *"And let the peace of God rule in your hearts, to the which also ye are called in one body; and be ye thankful. Let the word of Christ dwell in you richly in all wisdom; teaching and admonishing one another in psalms and hymns and spiritual songs, singing with grace in your hearts to the Lord. And whatsoever ye do in word or deed, do all in the name of the Lord Jesus, giving thanks to God and the Father by him."*

Praising God is so essential that an entire book of praise was included in Scripture, and it's not just any kind of music. Multiple times it is stated to sing a new song unto the Lord, as we see in Isaiah 42:10-12, *"Sing unto the LORD a new song, and his praise from the end of the earth, ye that go down to the sea, and all that is therein; the isles, and the inhabitants thereof. Let the wilderness and the cities thereof lift up their voice, the villages that Kedar doth inhabit: let the inhabitants of the rock sing, let them shout from the top of the mountains. Let them give glory unto the LORD, and declare his praise in the islands."*

There is not enough room in this devotional study to expound upon the praise that God deserves and requires. Your life should be an audible instrument of praise to God.

Years ago, I started a notebook that I entitled my Blessing Book. I could only record God's blessings in it, not prayers, not worries, nothing but blessings. You would think that the book would be filled by now and multiple volumes to follow. Sadly, this book only has a few pages inscribed upon it. Not because God hasn't blessed, but because I do not take the time to praise Him by writing those blessings down.

Another definition was presented as "shining." Does praising God make you shine His light in your life? Think about how many examples of praising God in dark trials have been given in Scripture. Let your light so shine before men!

Are your thoughts full of praise? Think upon THESE things!

Philippians 4:7-9, *"And the peace of God, which passeth all understanding, shall keep your hearts and minds through Christ Jesus. Finally, brethren, whatsoever things are true, whatsoever things are honest, whatsoever things are just, whatsoever things are pure, whatsoever things are lovely, whatsoever things are of good report; if there be any virtue, and if there be any praise, think on these things. Those things, which ye have both learned, and received, and heard, and seen in me, do: and the God of peace shall be with you."*

Right now, I am taking the time to write down my praises in my blessing book. Will you take time to praise Him too?

You can start here:

_____

_____

_____

_____

Ingots of Influence

While writing my third novel, the subject matter delves into the influences in our lives. It became increasingly obvious to me that what we treasure influences our lives. Let's look at how these influences shape us into our current selves.

An ingot is defined as the mass of metal that has been cast into a size or shape that is convenient for storage, transportation, or work. It is usually semi-finished or finished in its intended form. We are all ingots of what we treasure. Are we a finished product, or is the Master Designer still molding us into the final vessel fit for His use?

Take a few moments and read Ezekiel 28 as it is a very picturesque illustration of what happened to Satan and many others who let pride and riches shape and influence them.

Ephesians 5 gives us clarity on what we should allow to shape and influence us. Let's look at this passage together: *"Be ye therefore followers of God, as dear children; And walk in love, as Christ also hath loved us, and hath given himself for us an offering and a sacrifice to God for a sweetsmelling savour. But fornication, and all uncleanness, or covetousness, let it not be once named among you, as becometh saints; Neither filthiness, nor foolish talking, nor jesting, which are not convenient: but rather giving of thanks. For this ye know, that no whoremonger, nor unclean person, nor covetous man, who is an idolater, hath any inheritance in the kingdom of Christ and of God. Let no man deceive you with vain words: for because of these things cometh the wrath of God upon the children of disobedience. Be not ye therefore partakers with them. For ye were sometimes darkness, but now are ye light in the Lord: walk as children of light: (For the fruit of the Spirit is in all goodness and righteousness and truth;) Proving what is acceptable unto the Lord. And have no fellowship with the unfruitful works of darkness, but rather reprove them. For it is a shame even to speak of those things which are done of them in secret. But all things that are reproved are made manifest by the light: for whatsoever doth make manifest is light. Wherefore he saith, Awake thou that sleepest, and arise from the dead, and Christ shall give thee light. See then that ye walk circumspectly, not as fools, but as wise, Redeeming the time, because the days are evil."* Ephesians 5:1-16.

Are you a pure ingot void of any imperfection and dross, or are you letting the influences of the world mold you and shape you into their image?

Write down what influences you each day:

_____

_____

_____

_____

Verdant Splendor

"And why take ye thought for raiment? Consider the lilies of the field, how they grow; they toil not, neither do they spin: And yet I say unto you, That even Solomon in all his glory was not arrayed like one of these. Wherefore, if God so clothe the grass of the field, which to day is, and to morrow is cast into the oven, shall he not much more clothe you, O ye of little faith? Therefore take no thought, saying, What shall we eat? or, What shall we drink? or, Wherewithal shall we be clothed? (For after all these things do the Gentiles seek:) for your heavenly Father knoweth that ye have need of all these things. But seek ye first the kingdom of God, and his righteousness; and all these things shall be added unto you. Take therefore no thought for the morrow: for the morrow shall take thought for the things of itself. Sufficient unto the day is the evil thereof." Matthew 6:28-34

Is your "to-do" list out of control? Feeling overwhelmed by all that you want or need to accomplish? Does society or even your sphere of influence dictate how you think and act? Scripture, throughout time, has reminded us to seek what pleases God first and in all things. This devotional study book is themed around what treasures should be in our heart and thus illustrated in our words and deeds.

Looking at the passage above, a field of flowers comes to my imagination. You can picture how lovely a meadow or garden is, it often brings a sense of beauty maybe even tranquility to the forefront. Our Heavenly Father sure knows how to make lush, vibrant, verdant beauty, and yet we worry about what we are going to eat or wear, or how we are going to make it through the day.

This passage reminds us that the riches of God's mercy and grace are more than even what King Solomon had, and that

God cares for His creation and His creatures. If God will take the time to make His creation so beautiful knowing that it's so fragile and temporary, do you not trust Him to clothe you in His beauty and array you in His splendor? If you can see the treasure in the fields, how much more treasure will you find in His field of service?

What are you seeking today, treasure fit for His Kingdom, or trends that will vanish quickly with time?

Today's Treasure to unearth:

_____

_____

_____

_____

_____

_____

Trends that I need to bury:

_____

_____

_____

_____

_____

_____

Banished Treasure

While reading a devotional book, I came across this phrase, "banished treasure," but it was used in reference to those who have gone to Heaven before us. It was focused on how to deal with our temporary sorrow and grief. The word "banished" did not fit the theme. However, it did give serious depth for study for this devotional. What would banished treasure actually be?

Banished means to be sent away, as official punishment, judgment. The only treasure that we truly have is what we do for Christ, and the souls that go to Heaven because of our witness and testimony.

When you put these two meanings together, banished treasure would be the loved ones or people who refuse Christ and are banished to hell. Let's get really forthright and talk about our witness, our testimony.

Are we sharing the treasures of God's Word, His Gospel to our loved ones? Will our sphere of influence be such that many will accept Christ because they want what we have? There is no such thing as an undercover Christian.

There are a couple of verses in the Bible that strike holy fear into our hearts *"Not every one that saith unto me, Lord, Lord, shall enter into the kingdom of heaven; but he that doeth the will of my Father which is in heaven. Many will say to me in that day, Lord, Lord, have we not prophesied in thy name? and in thy name have cast out devils? and in thy name done many wonderful works? And then will I profess unto them, I never knew you: depart from me, ye that work iniquity."* Matthew 7:21-23.

We live surrounded by a pseudo-Christianity that is often referred to as "Churchianity." Scripture describes it like this: *"This know also, that in the last days perilous times shall come. For men shall be lovers of their own selves, covetous, boasters, proud, blasphemers, disobedient to parents, unthankful, unholy, Without natural affection, trucebreakers, false accusers, incontinent, fierce, despisers of those that are good, Traitors, heady, highminded, lovers of pleasures more than lovers of God; Having a form of godliness, but denying the power thereof: from such turn away. For of this sort are they which creep into houses, and lead captive silly women laden with sins, led away with divers lusts, Ever learning, and never able to come to the knowledge of the truth.* " 2 Timothy 3:1-7.

Which category are you in today? Will you or your friends, family, or neighbors be banished from God's Presence for all eternity? *"And I saw a great white throne, and him that sat on it, from whose face the earth and the heaven fled away; and there was found no place for them. And I saw the dead, small and great, stand before God; and the books were opened: and another book was opened, which is the book of life: and the dead were judged out of those things which were written in the books, according to their works. And the sea gave up the dead which were in it; and death and hell delivered up the dead which were in them: and they were judged every man according to their works. And death and hell were cast into the lake of fire. This is the second death. And whosoever was not found written in the book of life was cast into the lake of fire."* Revelation 20:11-15

Who did I share Christ with today?

King's Ransom

"I am the rose of Sharon, and the lily of the valleys. As the lily among thorns, so is my love among the daughters. As the apple tree among the trees of the wood, so is my beloved among the sons. I sat down under his shadow with great delight, and his fruit was sweet to my taste. He brought me to the banqueting house, and his banner over me was love." Song of Songs 2:1-4

What a beautiful poetic picture of the love of God towards His bride. However, this bride is the body of believers whom He had to redeem from the bondage and slavery of sin. Throughout Scripture, we see that Jesus, the High King of Heaven, was destined before the foundation of the world to be our Ransom.

"For God so loved the world, that he gave his only begotten Son, that whosoever believeth in him should not perish, but have everlasting life. For God sent not his Son into the world to condemn the world; but that the world through him might be saved." John 3:16-17.

"Behold, what manner of love the Father hath bestowed upon us, that we should be called the sons of God: therefore the world knoweth us not, because it knew him not. Beloved, now are we the sons of God, and it doth not yet appear what we shall be: but we know that, when he shall appear, we shall be like him; for we shall see him as he is. And every man that hath this hope in him purifieth himself, even as he is pure." 1 John 3:1-3.

Do you feel the love? God is LOVE; He sent His beloved Son to be our ransom because He loved us. How do we know He loves us? *"Herein is love, not that we loved God, but that he loved us, and sent his Son to be the propitiation for our sins. Beloved, if God so loved us, we ought also to love one another. No man hath seen God at any time. If we love one another, God dwelleth in us, and his love is perfected in us. Hereby know we that we dwell in him, and he in us, because he hath given us of his Spirit. And we have seen and do testify that the Father sent the Son to be the Saviour of the world. Whosoever shall confess that Jesus is the Son of God, God dwelleth in him, and he in God. And we have known and believed the love that God hath to us. God is love; and he that dwelleth in love dwelleth in God, and God in him. Herein is our love made perfect, that we may have boldness in the day of judgment: because as he is, so are we in this world. There is no fear in love; but perfect love casteth out fear: because fear hath torment. He that feareth is not made perfect in love. We love him, because he first loved us. If a man say, I love God, and hateth his brother, he is a liar: for he that loveth not his brother whom he hath seen, how can he love God whom he hath not seen? And this commandment have we from him, That he who loveth God love his brother also."* 1 John 4:10-21.

Scripture is God's love letter to us, demonstrating that our redemption has been bought by the Savior's loving sacrifice. Are you living as one who has been lovingly ransomed, or are you still in sin's bondage?

For A Song

I got it "for a song" usually implies that you received something for the equivalent of singing a song for it. What do you get when you have a song? Usually, you get a scrap of a song stuck in your head all day. Music is one of the most powerful outlets to express ourselves. There is literally music for any and every occasion, thought, situation, etc.

For a song, you get a reminder, a remedy, or a reassurance. Think about that for a minute or two. We often go to sleep at night with a song running through our minds, maybe nearly unnoticed, and we wake up with one. It's so vitally important what music we listen to, because it permeates our very being.

"Rejoice in the LORD, O ye righteous: for praise is comely for the upright. Praise the LORD with harp: sing unto him with the psaltery and an instrument of ten strings. Sing unto him a new song; play skilfully with a loud noise." Psalms 33:1-3.

Are you making melody in your heart to the Lord as you are commanded to in Ephesians? *"Let every thing that hath breath praise the LORD. Praise ye the LORD."* Psalms 150:6. Is our song comely, does it praise the Lord?

There is a precious saint who is waiting to cross over into her heavenly home. Music has become the very breath that keeps her going each day; the joy of the Lord is her strength. It is that reassurance that she is loved by her Father, the remedy for her pain, the reminder that in spite of her situation, it's only temporary.

What do YOU have for a song?

"Then sang Moses and the children of Israel this song unto the LORD, and spake, saying, I will sing unto the LORD, for he hath triumphed gloriously: the horse and his rider hath

he thrown into the sea. The LORD is my strength and song, and he is become my salvation: he is my God, and I will prepare him an habitation; my father's God, and I will exalt him." Exodus 15:1-2.

If you are not listening to the right song, then read this verse again: *"And he hath put a new song in my mouth, even praise unto our God: many shall see it, and fear, and shall trust in the LORD."* Psalms 40:3.

Sing His song, and you'll have exactly what you need: hope, help, health, and happiness.

May you have exactly what you need today, for a song.

Into the Depths

"Awake, awake, put on strength, O arm of the LORD; awake, as in the ancient days, in the generations of old. Art thou not it that hath cut Rahab, and wounded the dragon? Art thou not it which hath dried the sea, the waters of the great deep; that hath made the depths of the sea a way for the ransomed to pass over? Therefore the redeemed of the LORD shall return, and come with singing unto Zion; and everlasting joy shall be upon their head: they shall obtain gladness and joy; and sorrow and mourning shall flee away. I, even I, am he that comforteth you: who art thou, that thou shouldest be afraid of a man that shall die, and of the son of man which shall be made as grass..." Isaiah 51:9-12.

Many times, we feel we are in too deep; the water is over our heads, and we are sinking. It is here, in these depths, that we can find treasure. The passage above talks about the depths of the sea as the way for the ransomed to pass over. Did you catch that word "over?" It does not seem to make sense if you are in the depths to be able to then pass over into safety. But for the redeemed who have been ransomed by the King, this is an easy concept to fathom.

Launch out into the deep and see what treasures you can find. *"That Christ may dwell in your hearts by faith; that ye, being rooted and grounded in love, May be able to comprehend with all saints what is the breadth, and length, and depth, and height; And to know the love of Christ, which passeth knowledge, that ye might be filled with all the fulness of God. Now unto him that is able to do exceeding abundantly above all that we ask or think, according to the power that worketh in us, Unto him be glory in the church by Christ Jesus throughout all ages, world without end. Amen."* Ephesians 3:17-21.

Soak in these two passages, let them permeate your hearts, there is so much comfort and strength to be absorbed in these rich depths. Did you even grasp a portion of the treasures to be found when you searched the depths of God's riches to us, His ransomed?

"But God, who is rich in mercy, for his great love wherewith he loved us, Even when we were dead in sins, hath quickened us together with Christ, (by grace ye are saved;) And hath raised us up together, and made us sit together in heavenly places in Christ Jesus: That in the ages to come he might shew the exceeding riches of his grace in his kindness toward us through Christ Jesus. For by grace are ye saved through faith; and that not of yourselves: it is the gift of God: Not of works, lest any man should boast. For we are his workmanship, created in Christ Jesus unto good works, which God hath before ordained that we should walk in them." Ephesians 2:4-10.

The next time you feel overwhelmed or think you are drowning, dive into the depths of God's Word and search out the path through the sea of life that leads to Zion with joy and singing.

(Need a little extra buoyancy? Dive into Romans 8:39 and Romans 11:33.)

Filigree of Faith

Earlier in our treasure hunt, we touched and examined the facets of faith. Let's add some filigree to that precious jewel in our spiritual foundation. *"According to the grace of God which is given unto me, as a wise masterbuilder, I have laid the foundation, and another buildeth thereon. But let every man take heed how he buildeth thereupon. For other foundation can no man lay than that is laid, which is Jesus Christ. Now if any man build upon this foundation gold, silver, precious stones, wood, hay, stubble; Every man's work shall be made manifest: for the day shall declare it, because it shall be revealed by fire; and the fire shall try every man's work of what sort it is. If any man's work abide which he hath built thereupon, he shall receive a reward. If any man's work shall be burned, he shall suffer loss: but he himself shall be saved; yet so as by fire."* 1 Corinthians 3:10-15.

What is filigree? The dictionary defines it as intricately designed work that is often delicate and ornamental. It is made from gold, silver, or other fine metals. Our faith in Jesus Christ is described in the passage above; the ornamental work that is added to it throughout our lives should be abiding and fireproof.

Have you ever worn some delicate jewelry that did not stand the test of normal wear and tear? Our faith is often like that, it wavers and is fragile and of not much use even for just looking at. We read in Scripture that the trying of our faith worketh patience. However, I would dare say that most of our trials are not making us more patient, but instead, tarnishing what we thought was our sturdy faith.

Our filigree is often more carnal costume jewelry quality. Our faith is to be carefully built upon with the precious treasures from the Word of God, the growth that He bears into fruit as we stay connected to the Vine.

What filigree are you adding to your faith? *"Simon Peter, a servant and an apostle of Jesus Christ, to them that have obtained like precious faith with us through the righteousness of God and our Saviour Jesus Christ: Grace and peace be multiplied unto you through the knowledge of God, and of Jesus our Lord, According as his divine power hath given unto us all things that pertain unto life and godliness, through the knowledge of him that hath called us to glory and virtue: Whereby are given unto us exceeding great and precious promises: that by these ye might be partakers of the divine nature, having escaped the corruption that is in the world through lust. And beside this, giving all diligence, add to your faith virtue; and to virtue knowledge; And to knowledge temperance; and to temperance patience; and to patience godliness; And to godliness brotherly kindness; and to brotherly kindness charity. For if these things be in you, and abound, they make you that ye shall neither be barren nor unfruitful in the knowledge of our Lord Jesus Christ."* 2 Peter 1:1-9.

Come into the Storehouse

Where do you store your treasure, your valuables? A bank, a safety deposit box, the sock drawer? Maybe you have dug holes in your backyard, or used a hopefully impregnable safe to secure what you consider valuable. In our treasure hunt through God's Word, we find that when we hide His Word in our hearts, it will reveal His gospel for all the world to see. Our treasure is on full display; whether it is true treasure or worthless gaudy baubles, it will be revealed at the final accounting.

How do you get into the storehouse of God's richest treasures? The key is the promise that unlocks the door to His riches. This tabernacle of treasure, the House of Blessing is to be our residence. *"Those that be planted in the house of the LORD shall flourish in the courts of our God. They shall still bring forth fruit in old age; they shall be fat and flourishing; To shew that the LORD is upright: he is my rock, and there is no unrighteousness in him."* Psalms 92:13-15.

We want the riches of His grace and glory, we want the blessings, however, His storehouse, His tabernacle is often robbed and looted. How can this be?! Surely the King of the Ages can keep His treasure secure from looters? It, sadly, is looted from within! *"Will a man rob God? Yet ye have robbed me. But ye say, Wherein have we robbed thee? In tithes and offerings. Ye are cursed with a curse: for ye have robbed me, even this whole nation. Bring ye all the tithes into the storehouse, that there may be meat in mine house, and prove me now herewith, saith the LORD of hosts, if I will not open you the windows of heaven, and pour you out a blessing, that there shall not be room enough to receive it."* Malachi 3:8-10.

We as His heirs, His inheritance of glory, have the key, the promise. And yet we act like common thieves, breaking into

God's treasures and defacing His Tabernacle, His storehouse of blessings.

This storehouse is filled with great treasure to be spilled out into wealth untold, blessings beyond number, and yet we live as paupers because we refuse to be obedient children of God in our time, our talent, our tithe, and our trust.

Use your key of promise, your title, your position to add more treasure into God's storehouse, and you will be truly rich beyond your wildest dreams.

Below, tally up what you have to give to God, and see if He will not give you blessings for trusting Him with your:

Tithe: _____

Talent: _____

Time: _____

Trust: _____

Treasures Untold

"Wherefore we receiving a kingdom which cannot be moved, let us have grace, whereby we may serve God acceptably with reverence and godly fear:" Hebrews 12:28.

Lately, the words "immovable," "steadfast," and "still" have become lifelines to me as I traverse life's turbulent seas. The treasure of a kingdom that cannot be moved is invaluable. Are you a citizen of this immovable Kingdom? If you can emphatically say "YES!" then nothing shall move you, no matter how traumatic it might seem.

"But as it is written, Eye hath not seen, nor ear heard, neither have entered into the heart of man, the things which God hath prepared for them that love him. But God hath revealed them unto us by his Spirit: for the Spirit searcheth all things, yea, the deep things of God." 1 Corinthians 2:9-10.

We do not know what God has prepared for us, but we do know that when God prepares it, it will be for our good and His glory. He will reveal His treasures, His plan, His thoughts, and His purpose through the Holy Spirit in His time.

Oh, my fellow treasure hunter, don't let the entanglements of the world distract you from seeking true treasure. Keep your eye on the prize; walk with your King through the snares and traps that seek to unsettle and destroy you. The path is treacherous, but the map is designed by the Keeper of the treasure, the Keeper of your soul!

The very God who spoke these words to Moses for Israel is your God if you have received His gift of eternal life through Jesus Christ. *"Ye have seen what I did unto the Egyptians, and how I bare you on eagles' wings, and brought you unto myself. Now therefore, if ye will obey my voice indeed, and keep my covenant, then ye shall be a peculiar treasure unto me above all people: for all the earth is mine: And ye shall be unto me a kingdom of priests, and an holy nation."* Exodus 19:4-6.

Our treasure is truly untold; it cannot be measured, and the half has yet been told about what God will do with you and for you if you are willing to be obedient!

Treasures for the Heart

Here, in the very center of our treasure hunt, is the heart of the matter. What treasures are stored in your heart? Paul writes this to his churches, and thusly to us as the church, the bride of Christ.

"For I would that ye knew what great conflict I have for you, and for them at Laodicea, and for as many as have not seen my face in the flesh; That their hearts might be comforted, being knit together in love, and unto all riches of the full assurance of understanding, to the acknowledgement of the mystery of God, and of the Father, and of Christ; In whom are hid all the treasures of wisdom and knowledge. And this I say, lest any man should beguile you with enticing words. For though I be absent in the flesh, yet am I with you in the spirit, joying and beholding your order, and the stedfastness of your faith in Christ. As ye have therefore received Christ Jesus the Lord, so walk ye in him: Rooted and built up in him, and stablished in the faith, as ye have been taught, abounding therein with thanksgiving. Beware lest any man spoil you through philosophy and vain deceit, after the tradition of men, after the rudiments of the world, and not after Christ. For in him dwelleth all the fulness of the Godhead bodily. And ye are complete in him, which is the head of all principality and power..." Colossians 2:1-10.

Herein is our treasure: comforted hearts, full assurance, the wisdom and knowledge out of the richness of understanding, along with our steadfastness of faith in Jesus Christ.

As we collect treasure, it will be evident in our spiritual growth. We will display these verses: *"Howbeit we speak wisdom among them that are perfect: yet not the wisdom of this world, nor of the princes of this world, that come to nought: But we speak the wisdom of God in a mystery, even the hidden wisdom, which God ordained before the world unto our glory:*

Which none of the princes of this world knew: for had they known it, they would not have crucified the Lord of glory." 1 Corinthians 2:6-8.

The treasure within is evident by the radiance that bursts forth in living splendor around you. If you feel jaded, dull, or tarnished, look within your heart to see what your treasure is made from. The riches of this world can never compare to the eternal riches that come from having eternal treasures in your heart that money cannot buy and thieves cannot steal.

For where your treasure is, there will your heart be also.

Read again these passages and see if you have hidden them in your heart:

Matthew 6:19-23
Matthew 12:35

Collecting the Bounty

"Help, LORD; for the godly man ceaseth; for the faithful fail from among the children of men. They speak vanity every one with his neighbour: with flattering lips and with a double heart do they speak. The LORD shall cut off all flattering lips, and the tongue that speaketh proud things: Who have said, With our tongue will we prevail; our lips are our own: who is lord over us? For the oppression of the poor, for the sighing of the needy, now will I arise, saith the LORD; I will set him in safety from him that puffeth at him. The words of the LORD are pure words: as silver tried in a furnace of earth, purified seven times. Thou shalt keep them, O LORD, thou shalt preserve them from this generation for ever. The wicked walk on every side, when the vilest men are exalted." Psalms 12.

This Psalm is a perfect illustration of our thought treasure. Herein, we get the comparison of earthly riches versus heavenly treasures. The word bounty has a few different meaning – it's a price given, a reward for removing something unwanted, or giving liberally with generosity.

"Therefore I thought it necessary to exhort the brethren, that they would go before unto you, and make up beforehand your bounty, whereof ye had notice before, that the same might be ready, as a matter of bounty, and not as of covetousness. But this I say, He which soweth sparingly shall reap also sparingly; and he which soweth bountifully shall reap also bountifully. Every man according as he purposeth in his heart, so let him give; not grudgingly, or of necessity: for God loveth a cheerful giver. And God is able to make all grace abound toward you; that ye, always having all sufficiency in all things, may abound to every good work..." 2 Corinthians 9:5-8.

Looking up passages to illustrate these concepts, it's difficult to just use one or two verses. The Scriptures contain so much bounty for us to remove the decay of sin and embrace the fullness of life found in Jesus Christ. Dig your hearts and hands into this treasure box.

"And to make all men see what is the fellowship of the mystery, which from the beginning of the world hath been hid in God, who created all things by Jesus Christ: To the intent that now unto the principalities and powers in heavenly places might be known by the church the manifold wisdom of God, According to the eternal purpose which he purposed in Christ Jesus our Lord: In whom we have boldness and access with confidence by the faith of him. Wherefore I desire that ye faint not at my tribulations for you, which is your glory. For this cause I bow my knees unto the Father of our Lord Jesus Christ, Of whom the whole family in heaven and earth is named, That he would grant you, according to the riches of his glory, to be strengthened with might by his Spirit in the inner man; That Christ may dwell in your hearts by faith; that ye, being rooted and grounded in love, May be able to comprehend with all saints what is the breadth, and length, and depth, and height; And to know the love of Christ, which passeth knowledge, that ye might be filled with all the fulness of God. Now unto him that is able to do exceeding abundantly above all that we ask or think, according to the power that worketh in us, Unto him be glory in the church by Christ Jesus throughout all ages, world without end. Amen." Ephesians 3:9-21.

Collect THIS bounty!

Gold Digger

This title probably brought an unfavorable definition to your mind. Let's back up into history with it first, as there are two obvious meanings. The literal definition would be, of course, one who digs for gold. The old word for this person was "prospector." What an interesting word to use if you think about it. The person was looking for the prospect of finding gold!

What does this mean if you simplify it? They "HOPED" to find gold but knew it would require extreme effort in often extreme conditions. It required certain types of tools, knowledge, experience, and guidance, among many other things.

Let's dig for gold, are you ready?

"The law of the LORD is perfect, converting the soul: the testimony of the LORD is sure, making wise the simple. The statutes of the LORD are right, rejoicing the heart: the commandment of the LORD is pure, enlightening the eyes. The fear of the LORD is clean, enduring for ever: the judgments of the LORD are true and righteous altogether. More to be desired are they than gold, yea, than much fine gold: sweeter also than honey and the honeycomb. Moreover by them is thy servant warned: and in keeping of them there is great reward." Psalms 19:7-11.

Where are we digging for gold? In Scripture, because it is more to be desired than even the finest earthly gold. Why? When you keep His Word, there is great reward. Earlier thoughts have highlighted this importance, but are you truly taking the time, effort, and hard work to learn and memorize the Word of God?

Do you have gold fever? *"All scripture is given by inspiration of God, and is **profitable** for doctrine, for reproof, for correction, for instruction in righteousness: That the man of*

God may be perfect, throughly furnished unto **_all good works_**."
2 Timothy 3:16-17.

Did you catch those key phrases in there, profitable and all good works? Do you find studying the Word of God to be profitable to you? If you haven't looked at it this way before, you do not have gold fever. *"I beseech you, brethren, (ye know the house of Stephanas, that it is the firstfruits of Achaia, and that they have addicted themselves to the ministry of the saints,) That ye submit yourselves unto such, and to every one that helpeth with us, and laboureth."* 1 Corinthians 16:15-16.

When you have gold fever, you'll be addicted to the ministry, you'll labor hard to win that prize. *"But <u>continue</u> thou in the things which thou hast learned and hast been assured of, knowing of whom thou hast learned them; And that from a child thou hast known the holy scriptures, which are able to make thee wise unto salvation through faith which is in Christ Jesus."* 2 Timothy 3:14-15. How can you continue in something if you have not even started? What does 2 Timothy 2:15 say? *"**Study** to shew thyself approved unto God, a **workman** that needeth not to be ashamed, rightly dividing the word of truth."* 2 Timothy 2:15.

Now, the other meaning of gold digger is someone who connected themselves to the one who had all the money, found the gold, and did the work and extorts them, steals from them, or expects them to take care of them so that they don't have to work.

Sadly, we treat pastors, teachers, and leaders in the church this way. It's true. We expect them to study and work hard learning Scripture, while we sit back and expect to be fed and our needs supplied by them!

Which gold digger are you?

Claim Jumper

A devotional excerpt stated that yesterday's victories are today's incentives for better enrichment. Too many times, we let someone rob us of our joy, our faith, our hope; they jump our claim spiritually. If you are a gold digger, as we previously discussed, it will be evident as to which one you are by how you protect your claim.

*"My brethren, count it all joy when ye fall into divers temptations; Knowing this, that the **trying** of your faith worketh patience. But let patience have her perfect **work**, that ye may be perfect and entire, **wanting nothing**. If any of you lack wisdom, let him ask of God, that **giveth to all men liberally**, and upbraideth not; and it shall be given him. But let him ask in faith, nothing wavering. For he that wavereth is like a wave of the sea driven with the wind and tossed. For let not that man think that he shall receive any thing of the Lord. A double minded man is unstable in all his ways. Let the brother of low degree rejoice in that he is exalted: <u>But the rich, in that he is made low</u>: because as the flower of the grass he shall pass away. For the sun is no sooner risen with a burning heat, but it withereth the grass, and the flower thereof falleth, and the grace of the fashion of it perisheth: <u>so also shall the rich man fade away in his ways.</u> **Blessed is the man that endureth temptation: for when he is tried, he shall receive the crown of life, which the Lord hath promised to them that love him.**"* James 1:2-12.

Highlighting certain points in this passage of Scripture makes them leap out at you. It requires faith and work, the generosity of God's grace, a humble spirit, and enduring every trial and temptation to receive the reward.

Are you protecting your claim? A story from the Old Testament readily comes to mind: *"And after him was Shammah the son of Agee the Hararite. And the Philistines were gathered together into a troop, where was a piece of ground full of lentiles: and the people fled from the Philistines. But* **he stood in the midst of the ground, and defended it, and slew the Philistines: and the LORD wrought a great victory.** *"* 2 Samuel 23:11-12. Shammah stood and fought in his pea patch, and the LORD gave the victory.

"Ye did run well; who did hinder you that ye should not obey the truth? This persuasion cometh not of him that calleth you. A little leaven leaveneth the whole lump. I have confidence in you through the Lord, that ye will be none otherwise minded: but he that troubleth you shall bear his judgment, whosoever he be." Galatians 5:7-10

What is hindering you from obeying the truth of God's Word? Let God take care of those trying to jump your claim, your stand on the Word of God! Be steadfast, UNMOVABLE, always abounding in the WORK and WORD!

Looking Through the Loupe

What in the world is a loupe? Maybe you know it more as the jeweler's glass. The jeweler uses this powerful magnifying glass to inspect the jewels for inclusions, cracks, and impurities, and get this – the definition says, "hearts and arrows".

Loving jewelry is completely different than understanding the intricacies that go into what man considers valuable. A jeweler uses this special magnifier that is small; in fact, the higher the magnification the smaller the lens. Think about that spiritually for a minute. Our King of kings is to be so magnified that when we look at Him, we see nothing else because our complete focus is on His pure holiness.

Now most loupes are illuminated, as they magnify ten to twenty times what is seen normally. This is to bring into shining, clear focus even the smallest, finest details. A jeweler also inspects the fitting/setting that the jewel is placed into.

*"And he that **searcheth the hearts** knoweth what is the mind of the Spirit, because he maketh intercession for the saints according to the will of God. And we know that all things work together for good to them that love God, to them who are the called **according to his purpose.** For whom he did foreknow, he also did predestinate to be conformed to the image of his Son, that he might be the firstborn among many brethren. Moreover whom he did predestinate, them he also called: and whom he **called**, them he also justified: and whom he **justified**, them he also **glorified.** What shall we then say to these things? If God be for us, who can be against us?"* Romans 8:27-31.

The Master Jeweler is searching your heart. Is it fitting into HIS purpose? Are you bringing shining glory to Him? I am not trying to find some sort of nugget in Scripture that no one else has seen. I am just trying to shine the illuminated loupe on our lives and see how we magnify the King of kings.

"Then they that feared the LORD spake often one to another: and the LORD hearkened, and heard it, and a book of remembrance was written before him for them that feared the LORD, and that thought upon his name. And they shall be mine, saith the LORD of hosts, in that day when I make up my jewels; and I will spare them, as a man spareth his own son that serveth him. Then shall ye return, and discern between the righteous and the wicked, between him that serveth God and him that serveth him not." Malachi 3:16-18.

This passage is a perfect illustration of what our Master Jeweler does with His loupe. He appraises our value.

Here is our response, our way of reflecting His illuminating magnification back to Him. Our praise value: *"I will bless the LORD at all times: his praise shall continually be in my mouth. My soul shall make her boast in the LORD: the humble shall hear thereof, and be glad. O magnify the LORD with me, and let us exalt his name together."* Psalms 34:1-3.

"For we are his workmanship, created in Christ Jesus unto good works, which God hath before ordained that we should walk in them." Ephesians 2:10.

In Plain Sight

On occasion, you'll hear a story of someone who was just walking along and found a precious jewel right there in plain sight! Often it turns out to be a very valuable piece of stone by worldly measurements of value. Many heavenly treasures are hidden in plain sight. This sounds like an oxymoron, but it depends on what you define as treasure. What sort of heavenly treasures can be found here on earth?

Scripture has numerous stories of simple, often lowly people whom God used in a mighty, spectacular way. Their outward appearance may not have shown the treasures hidden within.

"But the LORD said unto Samuel, Look not on his countenance, or on the height of his stature; because I have refused him: for the LORD seeth not as man seeth; for man looketh on the outward appearance, but the LORD looketh on the heart." 1 Samuel 16:7-8.

Think about Rahab the harlot and Ruth the Moabitess; they did not seem to be much, but God used them to further His message of redemption. Think about the little servant maiden to Naaman's wife; she was instrumental in bringing about a miracle for her master. Then we have David, who was used mightily and was the legacy through which the Messiah came to earth! God chose fishermen and tax collectors and common people as His closest followers while on this earth. What then of the Apostle Paul? We meet him as murderous Saul, but God used him to be a missionary, and his example is beyond value to our ministry outreaches today.

All these were not used by how they looked, and most people would scoff at the idea of their value or worth by society's standards. Their treasure, their willingness to be found faithful, was hidden in plain sight.

What are some of the treasures we may find hidden in plain sight? Kindness, compassion, maybe wisdom, these are threads of gold and silver that run through our vessels of beauty and honor when we are in the Master's hands.

"Then Peter said, Silver and gold have I none; but such as I have give I thee: In the name of Jesus Christ of Nazareth rise up and walk. And he took him by the right hand, and lifted him up: and immediately his feet and ankle bones received strength. And he leaping up stood, and walked, and entered with them into the temple, walking, and leaping, and praising God. And all the people saw him walking and praising God: And they knew that it was he which sat for alms at the Beautiful gate of the temple: and they were filled with wonder and amazement at that which had happened unto him. And as the lame man which was healed held Peter and John, all the people ran together unto them in the porch that is called Solomon's, greatly wondering. And when Peter saw it, he answered unto the people, Ye men of Israel, why marvel ye at this? or why look ye so earnestly on us, as though by our own power or holiness we had made this man to walk?" Acts 3:6-12.

Are you a treasure hidden in plain sight? There are always people that God puts in our lives that are full of wisdom, kindness, or compassion, that may not be much to look at outwardly, but their inner beauty is like a rare, priceless gem. Are you looking for the heavenly treasures that can be found here on Earth?

Valuable Resources

"I can't do anything; God can't use me; I'm a mess!" Have you heard those words? Maybe you have even said or thought those words throughout your life. How can God use someone like me? In our previous treasure hunt, we saw how God does, indeed, use the unlikely sort of people to further His mission.

What are some of the resources that God has put in you that He can use or that He would like to use, when you are willing to be used?

"A good name is rather to be chosen than great riches, and loving favour rather than silver and gold. The rich and poor meet together: the LORD is the maker of them all." Proverbs 22:1-2.

"By humility and the fear of the LORD are riches, and honour, and life." Proverbs 22:4. Did you catch that? A good name, loving favour, humility, and the fear of the LORD are more to be treasured than silver and gold. Not only that, but the rich and the poor are on the same level in God's perspective.

Let's look again at the New Testament book of wisdom, so much like Proverbs is in the Old Testament.

"My brethren, count it all joy when ye fall into divers temptations; Knowing this, that the trying of your faith worketh patience. But let patience have her perfect work, that ye may be perfect and entire, wanting nothing. If any of you lack wisdom, let him ask of God, that giveth to all men liberally, and upbraideth not; and it shall be given him. But let him ask in faith, nothing wavering. For he that wavereth is like a wave of the sea driven with the wind and tossed. For let not that man think that he shall receive any thing of the Lord. A double minded man is unstable in all his ways. Let the brother of low degree rejoice in that he is exalted: But the rich, in that he is made low: because

as the flower of the grass he shall pass away. For the sun is no sooner risen with a burning heat, but it withereth the grass, and the flower thereof falleth, and the grace of the fashion of it perisheth: so also shall the rich man fade away in his ways." James 1:2-11.

Walk through that passage. What are the valuables you find there? Proverbs and James both say that wisdom comes from having the fear of the Lord, and with wisdom, we get understanding. *"The secret of the LORD is with them that fear him; and he will shew them his covenant."* Psalms 25:14.

The focus of value comes not in wealth but in the resources that you make available for your Master to use. Wisdom, kindness, compassion, faithfulness, all these are more precious than gold or silver that fades away.

"Every good gift and every perfect gift is from above, and cometh down from the Father of lights, with whom is no variableness, neither shadow of turning." James 1:17.

God is the One Who sees and makes you valuable – to Him!

That's Fine

Our English words are so muddled in usage, we tend to take words that mean value and devalue their meaning. The word "fine" for example, when used correctly is meant to describe the richest and highest quality of something. Scripture uses this correct definition repeatedly to ensure that we know that God uses the highest standards of purity that this earth can offer.

"I will make a man more precious than fine gold; even a man than the golden wedge of Ophir." Isaiah 13:12.

"How is the gold become dim! how is the most fine gold changed! the stones of the sanctuary are poured out in the top of every street. The precious sons of Zion, comparable to fine gold, how are they esteemed as earthen pitchers, the work of the hands of the potter!" Lamentations 4:1-2.

However, when we devalue God's creation and heap to ourselves pride, we become poor quality. The highest quality of treasure comes when the precious stones are carefully cut and polished through the hands of the Master Craftsman. The hottest fires try the most precious metal.

Yet today, we use the word "fine" to mean just okay, fair to middling, a way to deflect how we actually feel. When you say you are "fine," are you saying that God is working patience through your unmovable faith to produce a workman that needeth not to be ashamed? No, more often than not, we are just saying words out of politeness with no meaning, and the recipient of those words does not truly care how you are actually feeling or doing.

Heavenly treasures are not being collected and stored for all eternity because we no longer value them. We seek to just plod along through life's winding, turbulent way and hope we survive. The mere thought of having life and having it more abundantly seems too far out of our reach. The finest things in life seem to only go to those who are wealthy enough to afford them. We view spiritual treasures the same way; only super Christians, the missionaries, preachers, leaders etc. can have the blessings. We, the common people, have to settle for scraps that they might drop from the Master's table.

"Happy is the man that findeth wisdom, and the man that getteth understanding. For the merchandise of it is better than the merchandise of silver, and the gain thereof than fine gold. She is more precious than rubies: and all the things thou canst desire are not to be compared unto her. Length of days is in her right hand; and in her left hand riches and honour. Her ways are ways of pleasantness, and all her paths are peace. She is a tree of life to them that lay hold upon her: and happy is every one that retaineth her." Proverbs 3:13-18.

Our recent thoughts have been on the precious value of wisdom. *"The law of the LORD is perfect, converting the soul: the testimony of the LORD is sure, making wise the simple. The statutes of the LORD are right, rejoicing the heart: the commandment of the LORD is pure, enlightening the eyes. The fear of the LORD is clean, enduring for ever: the judgments of the LORD are true and righteous altogether. More to be desired are they than gold, yea, than much fine gold: sweeter also than honey and the honeycomb. Moreover by them is thy servant warned: and in keeping of them there is great reward."* Psalms 19:7-11.

Now That's FINE!

Low Tide

More often than not, a storm will cause a shipwreck, and the precious cargo is lost to the depths of the sea. Treasure hunters excitedly look for lost treasure from ages past. There is no thought of the lives lost, only the recovery of the precious cargo.

Our lives are often the same way: a storm arises, and we might lose faith or precious growth that we think has matured us. So much of our precious treasure is seemingly lost to the waves of life's turbulent seas. Is all lost? Our family and friends often do not seem to understand the depth of the situation. They do not feel how the stormy seas batter us and leave us feeling discouraged. Take courage, my friend, be as David, and encourage yourself in the Lord!

Why would you give up on recovering precious treasure? You can't hunt for treasure or recover what is lost during the raging of the storm. However, most treasure is often found washed ashore after the storm. Low tide will often reveal treasures for those seeking them. We can view this time in our lives as a shipwreck and a total loss, or we can seek to recover and collect what is often revealed once the storm has passed.

"God is our refuge and strength, a very present help in trouble. Therefore will not we fear, though the earth be removed, and though the mountains be carried into the midst of the sea; Though the waters thereof roar and be troubled, though the mountains shake with the swelling thereof. Selah. There is a river, the streams whereof shall make glad the city of God, the holy place of the tabernacles of the most High. God is in the midst of her; she shall not be moved: God shall help her, and that right early." Psalms 46:1-5.

This passage reminds us Who our refuge is in the storms of life; we do not have to be moved or shipwrecked no matter how turbulent life becomes. Any true treasure that is worth collecting for the kingdom of God will always be found again, should we find ourselves feeling like we are lost at sea.

The storm will not rage forever; there will come a time of low tide where you can catch your breath and explore the treasures that have washed ashore. Take inventory of your treasures. They may not actually lost at sea; maybe, you just need to wait until the storm passes by.

"Be still, and know that I am God: I will be exalted among the heathen, I will be exalted in the earth. The LORD of hosts is with us; the God of Jacob is our refuge. Selah." Psalms 46:10-11.

Is Time a Treasure?

We do not know how much time we have here on this side of Heaven. Time, thus indeed, should be counted as a treasure, as our lives are but a vapor according to Scripture. We think of special moments that happen that we want to always remember and visit in the re-telling of the stories. We call these precious moments or precious memories. Truly, time is a treasure.

How do you value time? Do you treasure it based upon selfish desires or upon Sovereign design? *"For all our days are passed away in thy wrath: we spend our years as a tale that is told. The days of our years are threescore years and ten; and if by reason of strength they be fourscore years, yet is their strength labour and sorrow; for it is soon cut off, and we fly away."* Psalms 90:9-10.

Our lives may be a short story; it truly does matter what we do and how we live. We have talked about how our lives have value; we are bought with a price; we are to glorify God in our bodies which He dwells within after salvation.

"So teach us to number our days, that we may apply our hearts unto wisdom." Psalms 90:12.

King Solomon wrote about how significant time is, even if it seems to be all vanity.

"To every thing there is a season, and a time to every purpose under the heaven: A time to be born, and a time to die; a time to plant, and a time to pluck up that which is planted; A time to kill, and a time to heal; a time to break down, and a time to build up; A time to weep, and a time to laugh; a time to mourn, and a time to dance; A time to cast away stones, and a time to gather stones together; a time to embrace, and a time to refrain from embracing; A time to get, and a time to lose; a time to keep, and a time to cast away; A time to rend, and a time to sew; a

time to keep silence, and a time to speak; A time to love, and a time to hate; a time of war, and a time of peace. What profit hath he that worketh in that wherein he laboureth?" Ecclesiastes 3:1-9.

Look down a few more verses in this same chapter: *"He hath made every thing beautiful in his time: also he hath set the world in their heart, so that no man can find out the work that God maketh from the beginning to the end. I know that there is no good in them, but for a man to rejoice, and to do good in his life. And also that every man should eat and drink, and enjoy the good of all his labour, it is the gift of God. I know that, whatsoever God doeth, it shall be for ever: nothing can be put to it, nor any thing taken from it: and God doeth it, that men should fear before him. That which hath been is now; and that which is to be hath already been; and God requireth that which is past. And moreover I saw under the sun the place of judgment, that wickedness was there; and the place of righteousness, that iniquity was there. I said in mine heart, God shall judge the righteous and the wicked: for there is a time there for every purpose and for every work."* Ecclesiastes 3:11-17.

Time is a treasure. Do you value it as you should?

From Trash to Treasure

One man's junk is another man's treasure. When we put this into a spiritual application, it does not seem to compute. However, we were on the world's trash heap when the Lord saw us as redeemable and valuable to Him. Salvation takes our filthy rags of righteousness and makes them into a regenerated, precious vessel fit for the King.

He then begins to fill us with heavenly treasure to replace the trash that we used to contain. The works of the flesh are replaced with the fruit of the Spirit. We collect the precious stones of patience, the gold and silver of faith and hope, and the heavenly currency of prayer. *"What? know ye not that your body is the temple of the Holy Ghost which is in you, which ye have of God, and ye are not your own? For ye are bought with a price: therefore glorify God in your body, and in your spirit, which are God's."* 1 Corinthians 6:19-20.

You become a reclaimed piece destroyed by the devil and sin, and He refits you for His Kingdom.

"But we are all as an unclean thing, and all our righteousnesses are as filthy rags; and we all do fade as a leaf; and our iniquities, like the wind, have taken us away. And there is none that calleth upon thy name, that stirreth up himself to take hold of thee: for thou hast hid thy face from us, and hast consumed us, because of our iniquities. But now, O LORD, thou art our father; we are the clay, and thou our potter; and we all are the work of thy hand." Isaiah 64:6-8.

"Then I went down to the potter's house, and, behold, he wrought a work on the wheels. And the vessel that he made of clay was marred in the hand of the potter: so he made it again another vessel, as seemed good to the potter to make it." Jeremiah 18:3-4.

Let's read again how valuable we are to the Lord. *"But we have this treasure in earthen vessels, that the excellency of the power may be of God, and not of us. We are troubled on every side, yet not distressed; we are perplexed, but not in despair; Persecuted, but not forsaken; cast down, but not destroyed; Always bearing about in the body the dying of the Lord Jesus, that the life also of Jesus might be made manifest in our body. For we which live are alway delivered unto death for Jesus' sake, that the life also of Jesus might be made manifest in our mortal flesh."* 2 Corinthians 4:7-11.

We are no more trash, but treasure.

Live a life holy acceptable unto God. That is what He values the most!

Ancient Treasure

"The merchants of Sheba and Raamah, they were thy merchants: they occupied in thy fairs with chief of all spices, and with all precious stones, and gold." Ezekiel 27:22.

As you read through Scripture, it is full of references to gold, silver, precious jewels, and costly perfumes and spices. Many of our spiritual applications are compared to these treasured items. For example, we have these verses:

"...for he is like a refiner's fire, and like fullers' soap: And he shall sit as a refiner and purifier of silver: and he shall purify the sons of Levi, and purge them as gold and silver, that they may offer unto the LORD an offering in righteousness. Then shall the offering of Judah and Jerusalem be pleasant unto the LORD, as in the days of old, and as in former years." Malachi 3:2-4.

This whole devotional is a spiritual application based upon treasure as we understand it even in an earthly base of riches and wealth.

When we look at the life of Christ, we see that it was surrounded with symbolic comparisons as well.

"When they saw the star, they rejoiced with exceeding great joy. And when they were come into the house, they saw the young child with Mary his mother, and fell down, and worshipped him: and when they had opened their treasures, they presented unto him gifts; gold, and frankincense, and myrrh." Matthew 2:10-12.

Much study has been given concerning these three gifts given to the baby Jesus and their use both at the time of birth and symbolically to His death. There is financial, religious, and medicinal value to each of these gifts. What can be discerned is that whether it was treasure brought to the Tabernacle or the Temple, or even to the infant Messiah, they brought their best!

The ancient people, whether small or great, understood the significance of bringing only the finest, purest, and best to God. Where have we lost that valued concept? Did we lose it with apathy, laziness, or selfish retention of treasure? "Give of the best to your Master, give…"

"And Jesus sat over against the treasury, and beheld how the people cast money into the treasury: and many that were rich cast in much. And there came a certain poor widow, and she threw in two mites, which make a farthing. And he called unto him his disciples, and saith unto them, Verily I say unto you, That this poor widow hath cast more in, than all they which have cast into the treasury: For all they did cast in of their abundance; but she of her want did cast in all that she had, even all her living." Mark 12:41-44.

We are probably at heart more like, dare we even say it – Judas?!

"Then took Mary a pound of ointment of spikenard, very costly, and anointed the feet of Jesus, and wiped his feet with her hair: and the house was filled with the odour of the ointment. Then saith one of his disciples, Judas Iscariot, Simon's son, which should betray him, Why was not this ointment sold for three hundred pence, and given to the poor? This he said, not that he cared for the poor; but because he was a thief, and had the bag, and bare what was put therein. Then said Jesus, Let her alone: against the day of my burying hath she kept this. For the poor always ye have with you; but me ye have not always." John 12:3-8.

These are indeed gifts fit for a King!

What treasure or the best of what you have are you giving to the Lord?

Fit For a King

Gold, frankincense, and myrrh were earthly gifts fit for our Heavenly King. Our King offers gifts to His joint heirs, such as salvation, joy, mercy, grace, hope, comfort, and an abundant life. These are such precious treasures, and so many more have been mentioned in our previous treasure hunts. Our lives should daily display the richness of His gifts to us.

What gift would you ask of God, were you to ask Him for anything? Most of us would probably immediately think of something financial and substantial. However, King Solomon was asked by God Himself what he would want if he could have anything in the world. King Solomon did not ask for riches as most earthly kings and even us common people would hope to receive. Instead, King Solomon asked for wisdom!

"In Gibeon the LORD appeared to Solomon in a dream by night: and God said, Ask what I shall give thee. And Solomon said, Thou hast shewed unto thy servant David my father great mercy, according as he walked before thee in truth, and in righteousness, and in uprightness of heart with thee; and thou hast kept for him this great kindness, that thou hast given him a son to sit on his throne, as it is this day. And now, O LORD my God, thou hast made thy servant king instead of David my father: and I am but a little child: I know not how to go out or come in. And thy servant is in the midst of thy people which thou hast chosen, a great people, that cannot be numbered nor counted for multitude. Give therefore thy servant an understanding heart to judge thy people, that I may discern between good and bad: for who is able to judge this thy so great a people? And the speech pleased the Lord, that Solomon had asked this thing. And God said unto him, Because thou hast asked this thing, and hast not asked for thyself long life; neither hast asked riches for thyself, nor hast asked the life of thine

enemies; but hast asked for thyself understanding to discern judgment; Behold, I have done according to thy words: lo, I have given thee a wise and an understanding heart; so that there was none like thee before thee, neither after thee shall any arise like unto thee. And I have also given thee that which thou hast not asked, both riches, and honour: so that there shall not be any among the kings like unto thee all thy days. And if thou wilt walk in my ways, to keep my statutes and my commandments, as thy father David did walk, then I will lengthen thy days." 1 Kings 3:5-14.

"So king Solomon exceeded all the kings of the earth for riches and for wisdom. And all the earth sought to Solomon, to hear his wisdom, which God had put in his heart." 1 Kings 10:23-24

Now, that was a gift fit for a king!

Live Like a King

Wisdom was a gift fit for a king, given by our King of kings. This royal gift is also given to the children of the King. We read in the book of James, often called the book of wisdom in the New Testament, that we, too, can have this gift. Many of us do not think of ourselves as living like royalty. However, we are too earthly-minded in most matters of value. *"Hearken, my beloved brethren, Hath not God chosen the poor of this world rich in faith, and heirs of the kingdom which he hath promised to them that love him?"* James 2:5.

"If any of you lack wisdom, let him ask of God, that giveth to all men liberally, and upbraideth not; and it shall be given him." James 1:5. This royal gift is offered to us, but how do we use it?

"The fear of the LORD is the beginning of wisdom: a good understanding have all they that do his commandments: his praise endureth for ever." Psalms 111:10. To live like a king is only possible when you let Jesus be King in your life. Fearing the Lord leads to wisdom, understanding, and discernment. This is what Solomon desired; it should be what we desire.

Let us see what the Old Testament book of wisdom tells us. *"The fear of the LORD is the beginning of knowledge: but fools despise wisdom and instruction. My son, hear the instruction of thy father, and forsake not the law of thy mother: For they shall be an ornament of grace unto thy head, and chains about thy neck."* Proverbs 1:7-9.

Wisdom, knowledge, instruction, all of these are to be desired, but only obtained when we fear the Lord. What does 'fear the Lord' mean to you? Are the standards of holy living so precious to you that you adorn yourself with them like jewelry?

"The fear of the LORD is the beginning of wisdom: and the knowledge of the holy is understanding. For by me thy days

shall be multiplied, and the years of thy life shall be increased." Proverbs 9:10-11.

Do you want to live like a king? Then live wisely in the fear of the Lord; let His Word instruct and guide every aspect of your life. *"But seek ye first the kingdom of God, and his righteousness; and all these things shall be added unto you."* Matthew 6:33

Regal Essence

The first treasure you ever collected was salvation. What a great gift the King of kings has given you. How did you receive this gift? You had to accept it by asking for it, right? You did this by an amazing avenue called prayer! This golden pathway leads straight to the Throne Room of God!

Prayer is so exceedingly precious that it adorns the very throne room in Heaven! Heaven is presented to us in various passages of Scripture as full of precious stones and priceless metals, along with unspeakable visions of splendor. However, when we are given the description of the very throne room of God Almighty, the closest thing to His throne is the altar. This altar is used in the book of Isaiah to purge Isaiah's unclean lips; it's used in the Tribulation for judgment. It is an integral part of God's divine display.

"And another angel came and stood at the altar, having a golden censer; and there was given unto him much incense, that he should offer it with the prayers of all saints upon the golden altar which was before the throne. And the smoke of the incense, which came with the prayers of the saints, ascended up before God out of the angel's hand." Revelation 8:3-4.

Did you catch that? The very essence of the throne room of God is an abundance of incense mixed with the prayers of all saints. Prayer is the very essence that comes before the nostrils of God! Prayer is a study that should take a lifetime to complete. Do you treasure prayer as much as God does?

Prayer, when it arrives in the throne room of God, can be seen, smelled, felt, and heard. Of all the costly perfumes that the King of all creation might have to perfume His throne room, the finest of flowers, odors, and costly perfumes, such as those given to Jesus upon earth, were not as precious to Him as the prayers of the saints!

Your prayers to God are a treasure to HIM! Prayer benefits the saints, but it blesses the very atmosphere of the Savior! What priceless perfume does He smell when you pray to Him today? Is it any wonder that Scripture tells us, *"Rejoice evermore. Pray without ceasing. In every thing give thanks: for this is the will of God in Christ Jesus concerning you."* 1 Thessalonians 5:16-18.

A Veritable Gold Mine

Many times in recent months, while compiling these nuggets of *Treasure For the Heart*, God would unearth yet another Scripture that went along with these thoughts. Whether in a devotional, or a Bible study, Sunday School, a song, or often in a sermon. Each time as more of the wealth of God's Word is displayed, it seems as if a veritable gold mine has been revealed.

Let's display some recent nuggets from various sources and see if they do not bring to mind recent thoughts from previous treasure hunts.

~There is no greater place for the Lord to be presented at His best than right in the midst of your storm.

~An altar of prayer is better than gold or silver.

~When I found a treasure in Jesus, I became rich beyond measure.

~Wisdom is a treasure in time. Are we treasuring His Word and obeying it?

~Tears are the diamonds of Heaven. (see next entry)

~Prayers are kept in a book in Heaven, that when the pages are turned, a waft of precious fragrance springs forth.

~Saints are His regal treasure, which He guards as the apple of His eye.

~Storms drive people to priceless mines of the Love of God in Christ.

~It was storms that unearthed the gold mines in India!

These thoughts were adapted and summarized from a devotional by Spurgeon and a devotional by L.B. Cowman. Repeatedly, God will display how treasures from His Word are vital to the Christian life.

"The sacrifice of the wicked is an abomination to the LORD: but the prayer of the upright is his delight." Proverbs 15:8.

"If thou seekest her as silver, and searchest for her as for hid treasures; Then shalt thou understand the fear of the LORD, and find the knowledge of God. For the LORD giveth wisdom: out of his mouth cometh knowledge and understanding. He layeth up sound wisdom for the righteous: he is a buckler to them that walk uprightly. He keepeth the paths of judgment, and preserveth the way of his saints. Then shalt thou understand righteousness, and judgment, and equity; yea, every good path." Proverbs 2:4-9.

When you search for treasure in God's Word, He will not only show it to you, but you will find a veritable gold mine to draw from!

Diamonds of Heaven

Whilst reading Revelation, we find how precious the prayers of the saints are to the Lord. We read of all the glorious beauty and wealth that is fit for our King of kings in His Heavenly realm. However, one author stated that tears are the diamonds of Heaven. What a precious way to describe how God cares for how we are feeling.

These are not the tears of a petulant tantrum from disappointment or anger. These are the precious tears that God hears and holds when His child cries out to Him with their very soul!

"In those days was Hezekiah sick unto death. And the prophet Isaiah the son of Amoz came to him, and said unto him, Thus saith the LORD, Set thine house in order; for thou shalt die, and not live. Then he turned his face to the wall, and prayed unto the LORD, saying, I beseech thee, O LORD, remember now how I have walked before thee in truth and with a perfect heart, and have done that which is good in thy sight. And Hezekiah wept sore. And it came to pass, afore Isaiah was gone out into the middle court, that the word of the LORD came to him, saying, Turn again, and tell Hezekiah the captain of my people, Thus saith the LORD, the God of David thy father, I have heard thy prayer, I have seen thy tears: behold, I will heal thee: on the third day thou shalt go up unto the house of the LORD." 2 Kings 20:1-5.

"My face is foul with weeping, and on my eyelids is the shadow of death; Not for any injustice in mine hands: also my prayer is pure. O earth, cover not thou my blood, and let my cry have no place. Also now, behold, my witness is in heaven, and my record is on high. My friends scorn me: but mine eye poureth out tears unto God." Job 16:16-20.

"Thou tellest my wanderings: put thou my tears into thy bottle: are they not in thy book? When I cry unto thee, then shall mine enemies turn back: this I know; for God is for me. In God will I praise his word: in the LORD will I praise his word. In God have I put my trust: I will not be afraid what man can do unto me." Psalms 56:8-11.

"...Seest thou this woman? I entered into thine house, thou gavest me no water for my feet: but she hath washed my feet with tears, and wiped them with the hairs of her head. Thou gavest me no kiss: but this woman since the time I came in hath not ceased to kiss my feet. My head with oil thou didst not anoint: but this woman hath anointed my feet with ointment. Wherefore I say unto thee, Her sins, which are many, are forgiven; for she loved much: but to whom little is forgiven, the same loveth little. And he said unto her, Thy sins are forgiven." Luke 7:44-48.

Our very tears are recorded in a book in Heaven, quite possibly kept in a celestial bottle, and are recognized by God as a fervent partner with our prayers. Dost thou not yet agree with the writer that they can be construed as Heavenly diamonds?

Exquisite Elixer

This adventure began by collecting spiritual treasures, something that we can store up in the Celestial Realm or take with us on our journey of spiritual growth. As you have looked at the various Scriptures highlighting the treasures to seek, it might become easy to just think of collecting and storing for later. However, these treasures are usable right here in the nasty now and now!

Many of these treasures are meant to be used on a minute-by-minute basis, yet there is one exquisite treasure that too often is overlooked or unused. Proverbs is one of those veritable gold mines with treasure in every verse. Go ahead, read Proverbs 15, and then, let's look at a few specific verses.

"A merry heart maketh a cheerful countenance: but by sorrow of the heart the spirit is broken." Proverbs 15:13. Realizing that a merry heart is a treasure might change how we react to the frustrations of life. After doing a bit of study upon the word "FRET," it seemed to be the hindering maelstrom too many Christians fall into. We fret more than we are merry.

F= Fearful
R= Reaction to
E= Every
T= Thing

This acrostic's reality was brought to mind, and thus, it needed an antidote! What sort of medicine would counteract the effects of fear, fretting, worry, and anxiety that so overwhelmingly pervades our society? Are we collecting the joy of the Lord, which is our strength? Are we being thankful instead of anxious, taking everything to the Lord in Prayer? As you read Proverbs 15:13, look over to verse 15. *"All the days of the afflicted are evil: but he that is of a merry heart hath a continual feast."* Proverbs 15:15. Maybe another similar verse comes to mind. *"A merry heart doeth good like a medicine: but a broken spirit drieth the bones."* Proverbs 17:22.

Sadly, even from Bible times until now, too many people get a merry heart or become merry after too much indulgence in fermented beverages. This merry heart is temporary and shallow. How much better is a merry heart that rejoices in the Lord always, for it is the exquisite eternal elixir that heals broken hearts, wounded spirits, and fretful worriers.

Just Store It!

"But lay up for yourselves treasures in heaven, where neither moth nor rust doth corrupt, and where thieves do not break through nor steal: For where your treasure is, there will your heart be also." Matthew 6:20-21.

Our key verses have emphasized the need for the right kind of treasure for the heart. However, we would be remiss if we did not look at another phrase in this passage. "Lay up" might make us think of the word "layaway," but lately, I have realized this is so much more about storing up treasures.

As a society, we are used to storing things, usually things that we do not use or need. Spiritually speaking, we tend to have the same habits; we store the things that we aren't using, no matter how much value they have. We tend to use the things that we should not even have in our possession.

We store trauma; instead of letting it heal, it just lays dormant until the next trigger brings it back to the forefront. We store up bitterness and malice and anger. Those are usually the first reactions we have to things that do not please us. Our "treasures" are collections of bad attitudes and hurt feelings.

"But as it is written, Eye hath not seen, nor ear heard, neither have entered into the heart of man, the things which God hath prepared for them that love him." 1 Corinthians 2:9.

It is one thing for us to store up spiritual treasures, but this Scripture says God has prepared unimaginable things for those who love Him. Think about what God has stored for each of us in His celestial storage units!

What do you have in your hand, friend? Is it worth using? Is it treasure that will constantly increase and fill up the storehouses of Heaven? *"It is of the LORD's mercies that we are not consumed, because his compassions fail not. They are new every morning: great is thy faithfulness. The LORD is my portion, saith my soul; therefore will I hope in him. The LORD is good unto them that wait for him, to the soul that seeketh him. It is good that a man should both hope and quietly wait for the salvation of the LORD."* Lamentations 3:22-26.

The Lord is my portion; oh, to mean this as the writer of old did. Is the Lord my portion? Are God and His way really enough?

Open the doors of your heart's storage, take inventory, and store up treasure that is pleasing the Lord. Get rid of all the evil treasures that will only corrupt your heart and mind. Let God be your portion!

The Restoration Process

Treasure-seeking often leads to deep, dark, dirty places to find the object that is priceless. Such is the same that our Savior did - He chose us to be His treasure! He came down to a wicked world to be Heaven's Priceless Pearl sacrificed on our eternal behalf.

As we treasure hunt through Scripture, we see that to repay Him for this redemptive treasure, we are to consider the reproach of Christ as greater riches than anything this world can offer. We must let the Savior enter our worthless vessel and clean it from the inside out. Then the treasure of this clean heart will be fellowship with God! As one preacher explained, this in itself has its own reward! *"That which we have seen and heard declare we unto you, that ye also may have fellowship with us: and truly our fellowship is with the Father, and with his Son Jesus Christ. And these things write we unto you, that your joy may be full."*

1 John 1:3-4 shows us that a clean heart leads to fellowship both with the Lord and with others. Once the darling Savior enters our heart, saves our soul, then cleanses us from the inside out, we are given the inexplicable treasure of true love. We learn what true love is and can then, in turn, love God and others with real love as commanded.

"And thou shalt love the Lord thy God with all thy heart, and with all thy soul, and with all thy mind, and with all thy strength: this is the first commandment. And the second is like, namely this, Thou shalt love thy neighbour as thyself. There is none other commandment greater than these." Mark 12:30-31. We are unable to do this completely without first having His true love dwelling within us.

The small books of 1 John, 2 John, and 3 John are such treasure troves about how to have the treasure of a clean heart that makes fellowship with God something that we crave more than any earthly treasure. These books tell us what the love of God is really all about and how it is our privilege to be the showpieces in His eternal display case of such immeasurable treasure that He bestows upon us.

God calls you His treasure. He wants to redeem you, clean you up, restore you, and display you to others who need Him too. Then, as Jude so eloquently stated, *"But ye, beloved, building up yourselves on your most holy faith, praying in the Holy Ghost, Keep yourselves in the love of God, looking for the mercy of our Lord Jesus Christ unto eternal life. And of some have compassion, making a difference: And others save with fear, pulling them out of the fire; hating even the garment spotted by the flesh. Now unto him that is able to keep you from falling, and to present you faultless before the presence of his glory with exceeding joy, To the only wise God our Saviour, be glory and majesty, dominion and power, both now and ever. Amen."* Jude 1:20-25.

Use the Dynamite!

Dunamis, the root word for dynamite, is the best word to describe the almighty power of God. Our words are so finite to describe such an awesome force. This power of God is a treasure for us, not just to see and fear, but it is actually given to us as Christians to help us, to strengthen us.

Thinking about all the Scripture that comes to mind about the power of God, it is of no wonder that you will find it all throughout our Bible! *"But we have this treasure in earthen vessels, that the excellency of the power may be of God, and not of us."* 2 Corinthians 4:7. This passage is one of the core passages near and dear to my heart, and such treasure to collect, and yet the treasure of the power of God has not even been mined heretofore.

Did other Scripture come to your mind about the power of God? Let us mine the Word of God together for the next little while and see what treasure we collect.

"Behold that which I have seen: it is good and comely for one to eat and to drink, and to enjoy the good of all his labour that he taketh under the sun all the days of his life, which God giveth him: for it is his portion. Every man also to whom God hath given riches and wealth, and hath given him power to eat thereof, and to take his portion, and to rejoice in his labour; this is the gift of God. For he shall not much remember the days of his life; because God answereth him in the joy of his heart." Ecclesiastes 5:18-20.

"But as many as received him, to them gave he power to become the sons of God, even to them that believe on his name:" John 1:12.

Power is a gift from God to receive salvation, to live for the Lord, and to proclaim His Gospel to the lost. *"...And he said, I am Jesus whom thou persecutest. But rise, and stand upon thy feet: for I have appeared unto thee for this purpose, to make thee a minister and a witness both of these things which thou hast seen, and of those things in the which I will appear unto thee; Delivering thee from the people, and from the Gentiles, unto whom now I send thee, To open their eyes, and to turn them from darkness to light, and from the power of Satan unto God, that they may receive forgiveness of sins, and inheritance among them which are sanctified by faith that is in me."* Acts 26:15-18.

"But ye shall receive power, after that the Holy Ghost is come upon you: and ye shall be witnesses unto me both in Jerusalem, and in all Judaea, and in Samaria, and unto the uttermost part of the earth." Acts 1:8.

Don't foolishly think that you generate this power; all power belongs to God, yet He uses it to strengthen us.

Your turn to mine for the dunamis in Scripture:

Write down the power that you find in these references:

1 Corinthians 2:5 - _____

1 Corinthians 4:20 - _____

2 Timothy 1:7 - _____

1 Peter 1:5 - _____

On A Silver Platter

"On a silver platter" is an idiom we often use in derision when someone seems to get something of great value without having worked for it. Think about this! Our entire life in Christ is given to us on a silver platter. We did nothing to deserve, earn, or work for our salvation! It is a gift of God; we must simply believe and receive it!

Blessings are given to us on a silver platter. Do we sniff in disdain and jealousy when others seem to get all the blessings and we are left feeling frustrated under our supposed burdens? During this treasure hunt, it has been obvious that every treasure we find in Scripture for our hearts to use here on earth or to store up in Heaven is given to us "on a silver platter."

Silver platters were a symbol of wealth and distinction, do we not serve the King of kings, Who owns the cattle on a thousand hills? Think about this, the idiom has the meaning of service. Are you a faithful steward of what you have been given?

Our Lord gave forth a parable about stewards, those given the position to maintain and invest in His work. Scripture also commands that the pastor be a faithful steward.

"If any be blameless, the husband of one wife, having faithful children not accused of riot or unruly. "For a bishop must be blameless, as the steward of God; not selfwilled, not soon angry, not given to wine, no striker, not given to filthy lucre; But a lover of hospitality, a lover of good men, sober, just, holy, temperate; Holding fast the faithful word as he hath been taught, that he may be able by sound doctrine both to exhort and to convince the gainsayers." Titus 1:6-9.

God gives us so much wealth and treasure undeserved, unearned, and unmerited. It does not matter what position you hold in the service of God; be found faithful!

"Let a man so account of us, as of the ministers of Christ, and stewards of the mysteries of God. Moreover it is required in stewards, that a man be found faithful." 1 Corinthians 4:1-2.

You have been served up salvation and blessings innumerable, power, strength, help, hope, and so much more treasure all on a silver platter. Are you, in turn, serving yourself back up to God in His Service?

What is on your platter?

Coin Incidents

We equate treasure often with an accumulation of money or things of value that can be transferred into monetary increments. Our entire monetary system is based upon silver and gold. This currency can be used for the Kingdom of God, or it can be used for filthy lucre.

Let's look at some coin incidents in Scripture, as we see how the simple exchange of coins was involved in such epic situations.

"And Judah said unto his brethren, What profit is it if we slay our brother, and conceal his blood? Come, and let us sell him to the Ishmeelites, and let not our hand be upon him; for he is our brother and our flesh. And his brethren were content. Genesis Then there passed by Midianites merchantmen; and they drew and lifted up Joseph out of the pit, and sold Joseph to the Ishmeelites for twenty pieces of silver: and they brought Joseph into Egypt." Genesis 37:26-28.

Did you notice the betrayal by Joseph for twenty pieces of silver?

"And Jesus sat over against the treasury, and beheld how the people cast money into the treasury: and many that were rich cast in much. And there came a certain poor widow, and she threw in two mites, which make a farthing. And he called unto him his disciples, and saith unto them, Verily I say unto you, That this poor widow hath cast more in, than all they which have cast into the treasury: For all they did cast in of their abundance; but she of her want did cast in all that she had, even all her living." Mark 12:41-44.

What are you giving into the treasury of our Lord? Are you giving all you have and all you are?

Acts 3 begins with a well-known story of one who spent his life trying to get money, but Peter did not have silver or gold coins to give him. What did Peter have that was so much better than begging for coins all day long?

"But godliness with contentment is great gain. For we brought nothing into this world, and it is certain we can carry nothing out. And having food and raiment let us be therewith content. But they that will be rich fall into temptation and a snare, and into many foolish and hurtful lusts, which drown men in destruction and perdition. For the love of money is the root of all evil: which while some coveted after, they have erred from the faith, and pierced themselves through with many sorrows. But thou, O man of God, flee these things; and follow after righteousness, godliness, faith, love, patience, meekness. Fight the good fight of faith, lay hold on eternal life, whereunto thou art also called, and hast professed a good profession before many witnesses." 1 Timothy 6:6-12.

We see in our final coin incident, this truth illustrated so devastatingly to the one who craved the filthy lucre:

"Then one of the twelve, called Judas Iscariot, went unto the chief priests, And said unto them, What will ye give me, and I will deliver him unto you? And they covenanted with him for thirty pieces of silver. And from that time he sought opportunity to betray him." Matthew 26:14-16.

Now look up Matthew 27:3-10 on your own and see the results of this coin incident!

Do you see how similar the story of Joseph was to this one?

Judah and Judas both betrayers or the nameless widow who gave all she had into the treasury; which one are you?

At Faith Value

Previously, we looked at the many facets of faith, the faces of faith presented to us in Hebrews 11. Throughout Scripture, the golden thread of faith weaves every story, every character into a beautiful tapestry of trusting God no matter the circumstances. Do we live our lives on a surface faith, taking it at face value, or do we dig down deeper and live at faith's value?

In the book of Genesis, we read of our first examples of faith, from Abraham to Moses, but in between, we have the story of Joseph. From the pit to the palace, this was not obtainable by mere chance or surface faith. Joseph truly had to deeply trust God and His promise given in a childhood vision.

"And the LORD was with Joseph, and he was a prosperous man; and he was in the house of his master the Egyptian. And his master saw that the LORD was with him, and that the LORD made all that he did to prosper in his hand. And Joseph found grace in his sight, and he served him: and he made him overseer over his house, and all that he had he put into his hand." Genesis 39:2-4.

Does your faith in the Lord show to those around you? This man, Joseph, was a slave in a foreign land, but that situation did not prevent him from trusting the Lord and serving Him.

"But the LORD was with Joseph, and shewed him mercy, and gave him favour in the sight of the keeper of the prison. And the keeper of the prison committed to Joseph's hand all the prisoners that were in the prison; and whatsoever they did there, he was the doer of it. The keeper of the prison looked not to any thing that was under his hand; because the LORD was with him, and that which he did, the LORD made it to prosper." Genesis 39:21-23.

Now, Joseph was framed, innocent of the crime he was accused of, and put in prison. Did this cause him to stop trusting God? NO!

"And Pharaoh said unto his servants, Can we find such a one as this is, a man in whom the Spirit of God is? And Pharaoh said unto Joseph, Forasmuch as God hath shewed thee all this, there is none so discreet and wise as thou art: Thou shalt be over my house, and according unto thy word shall all my people be ruled: only in the throne will I be greater than thou. And Pharaoh said unto Joseph, See, I have set thee over all the land of Egypt. And Pharaoh took off his ring from his hand, and put it upon Joseph's hand, and arrayed him in vestures of fine linen, and put a gold chain about his neck; And he made him to ride in the second chariot which he had; and they cried before him, Bow the knee: and he made him ruler over all the land of Egypt. And Pharaoh said unto Joseph, I am Pharaoh, and without thee shall no man lift up his hand or foot in all the land of Egypt. And Pharaoh called Joseph's name Zaphnathpaaneah; and he gave him to wife Asenath the daughter of Potipherah priest of On. And Joseph went out over all the land of Egypt." Genesis 41:38-45.

His faith in God's promise sent him straight to the palace, where this promise was fulfilled by God, in God's timing, through God's testing and training. Look at your life, dear one, is it lived at faith value?

That's Substantial!

Whilst we study the facets and deeper value of faith, let us broaden the beautiful spectrum of this jeweled treasure of the heart. *"Now faith is the substance of things hoped for, the evidence of things not seen."* Hebrews 11:1. This word **substance**, a very real and tangible object, is also defined as having great wealth and possessions! Think about this: every time the word **substance** is used in Scripture, it's about great wealth and very real tangible possessions. Why would we then not want to see the great wealth that can be found in having faith? Faith is the very evidence that what we hope for is real and tangible!

Faith is our Heavenly inheritance. Is that not what we are doing by storing up treasures in Heaven, exercising our faith, our very real and tangible belief that says God is truth and in Him is no lie?

If the word substance means to subsist by itself or a means of living, an inheritance, what a beautiful way to describe the treasure of faith. Faith in God is substance! Look at what the writer of Hebrews says in the previous chapter, *"For ye had compassion of me in my bonds, and took joyfully the spoiling of your goods, knowing in yourselves that ye have in heaven a better and an enduring substance. Cast not away therefore your confidence, which hath great recompence of reward. For ye have need of patience, that, after ye have done the will of God, ye might receive the promise. For yet a little while, and he that shall come will come, and will not tarry. Now the just shall live by faith: but if any man draw back, my soul shall have no pleasure in him. But we are not of them who draw back unto perdition; but of them that believe to the saving of the soul."* Hebrews 10:34-39.

As Scripture puts it, faith, even the smallest of faith, is substantial, not just in size, but in worth, value substance!

The very thought of it should overwhelm your senses with the wealth of the Celestial offered to you on a tangible promise. Your inheritance, incorruptible, that fadeth not away – now THAT's Substantial!

Diamond Jubilee

A Diamond Jubilee is a time of great celebration commemorating seventy-five years of commitment and dedication, usually in marriage, sometimes in business. The jewel chosen for this memorable occasion is the diamond. We have looked at diamonds before in our treasure hunt through Scripture. However, you might be interested to note that for the longest time, the most valuable diamond on earth was named the "Hope Diamond." It was renamed by the Hope family, who purchased it early on in its history. Even though it has changed owners through the centuries, it has never changed its name after being called the Hope Diamond.

Does this not make you draw lovely, spiritual parallels? Hope is a treasure we so earnestly seek; even Scripture says that if we have no hope, we are utterly at a loss. *"Hope deferred maketh the heart sick: but when the desire cometh, it is a tree of life."* Proverbs 13:12. Search through Scripture and find the vast wealth of verses about hope; what a prism they cast upon the walls of our hearts.

"O love the LORD, all ye his saints: for the LORD preserveth the faithful, and plentifully rewardeth the proud doer. Be of good courage, and he shall strengthen your heart, all ye that hope in the LORD." Psalms 31:23-24.

"Surely every man walketh in a vain shew: surely they are disquieted in vain: he heapeth up riches, and knoweth not who shall gather them. And now, Lord, what wait I for? my hope is in thee." Psalms 39:6-7.

Is your hope in riches or in the Lord? Just like the Hope Diamond is an immense and valuable gemstone, so our hope in the Lord needs to be immense, brilliant, and unchanging in its design as the years go by. Verse upon verse in the book of Psalms speaks of hope. There is so much mention of it, that it would definitely need to be in your cache of treasure for the heart.

"It is good that a man should both hope and quietly wait for the salvation of the LORD." Lamentations 3:26. Just like the Hope Diamond is considered of great value here on earth, so our hope must have great value to us. When our hope is in the Lord, we are thus rewarded both here on earth and in heaven for an eternal diamond jubilee.

"Looking for that blessed hope, and the glorious appearing of the great God and our Saviour Jesus Christ; Who gave himself for us, that he might redeem us from all iniquity, and purify unto himself a peculiar people, zealous of good works." Titus 2:13-14.

(On another interesting note, the Hope family also bought one of the largest pearls ever found and named it the Hope pearl – does that not remind you of how our hope is in the Pearl of Great Price, the Lord Jesus Christ?!)

Your Inheritance

"O thou afflicted, tossed with tempest, and not comforted, behold, I will lay thy stones with fair colours, and lay thy foundations with sapphires. And I will make thy windows of agates, and thy gates of carbuncles, and all thy borders of pleasant stones. And all thy children shall be taught of the LORD; and great shall be the peace of thy children. In righteousness shalt thou be established: thou shalt be far from oppression; for thou shalt not fear: and from terror; for it shall not come near thee. Behold, they shall surely gather together, but not by me: whosoever shall gather together against thee shall fall for thy sake. Behold, I have created the smith that bloweth the coals in the fire, and that bringeth forth an instrument for his work; and I have created the waster to destroy. No weapon that is formed against thee shall prosper; and every tongue that shall rise against thee in judgment thou shalt condemn. This is the heritage of the servants of the LORD, and their righteousness is of me, saith the LORD." Isaiah 54:11-17.

Whilst reading devotions this morning, this passage was highlighted, and the jewel of the agate was used as an illustration. With some research, you'll discover that the agate is usually formed under volcanic conditions. Our inheritance, O child of God, is formed here on earth by faith under intensely disruptive, chaotic conditions. Most jewels and gems are thusly formed in the earthly realm, even a pearl is formed from massive irritation to the oyster!

"Beloved, think it not strange concerning the fiery trial which is to try you, as though some strange thing happened unto you: But rejoice, inasmuch as ye are partakers of Christ's sufferings; that, when his glory shall be revealed, ye may be glad also with exceeding joy. If ye be reproached for the name of

Christ, happy are ye; for the spirit of glory and of God resteth upon you: on their part he is evil spoken of, but on your part he is glorified." 1 Peter 4:12-14.

Our trials of faith are fashioning us into the jewels that the Lord will use to make up His crown! Our inheritance is waiting for us in Heaven! Read that passage in Isaiah 54 again and take courage, dear one, our redemption draweth nigh!

Bank On It!

You can "take that to the bank," "bank on it," "got bank," all these are phrases used throughout the years to signify what? The bank was a building designed to hold, store, and secure things of value. Why would someone store their valued treasure in a bank? To put it simply, it was a place of trust! A bank is promoting itself as a trustworthy, secure location to keep and store what you treasure. What do you put your trust in?

It's obvious that people and places are not truly dependable, secure, and trustworthy, but Scripture always is. Our Father in Heaven, Jesus His Son, and the Holy Spirit are always trustworthy.

"But let all those that put their trust in thee rejoice: let them ever shout for joy, because thou defendest them: let them also that love thy name be joyful in thee." Psalms 5:11. Not only can you trust Him, but you can be happy while doing it!

"Shew thy marvellous lovingkindness, O thou that savest by thy right hand them which put their trust in thee from those that rise up against them. Keep me as the apple of the eye, hide me under the shadow of thy wings," Psalms 17:7-8.

He will keep you safe; He will treasure you as the valuable vessel that He is repairing and re-designing as His own. Scripture upon Scripture speaks of trust. I fear too many of us have not even dug into the depths of this treasure.

"And they that know thy name will put their trust in thee: for thou, LORD, hast not forsaken them that seek thee." Psalms 9:10. Psalm upon Psalm praises the Lord for being the only One we can trust. His faithfulness to usward is something you can surely take to the bank. But what about our trust in Him? Can He bank on that? When your Heavenly Father looks at you, does He see a faithful steward who trusts in Him? *"And David spake unto the LORD the words of this song in the day that the LORD*

had delivered him out of the hand of all his enemies, and out of the hand of Saul: And he said, The LORD is my rock, and my fortress, and my deliverer; The God of my rock; in him will I trust: he is my shield, and the horn of my salvation, my high tower, and my refuge, my saviour; thou savest me from violence. I will call on the LORD, who is worthy to be praised: so shall I be saved from mine enemies." 2 Samuel 22:1-4.

Take a few moments and continue reading 2 Samuel 22, and write down the things that you can trust about God, just as David did.

_____

_____

_____

"As for God, his way is perfect; the word of the LORD is tried: he is a buckler to all them that trust in him." 2 Samuel 22:31. A buckler is a shield used for hand-to-hand combat. When Scripture states that you can trust God, then you can truly Bank on IT!

Epiphany

Whilst on this treasure hunt, it became easy to focus on storing treasure or possibly trying to use it, but a vital part of this analogy is that these treasures are meant to be shared! When we put our trust in the eternal stronghold of God's Bank, we are thus given shares, a partnership to use and distribute His wealth to others. We tend to guard our hearts, but we don't always give our hearts to the Lord or to His Service. When we hoard treasure, we are not putting it to the use that it was intentionally given to us to serve Him.

"Therefore hath the LORD recompensed me according to my righteousness, according to the cleanness of my hands in his eyesight. With the merciful thou wilt shew thyself merciful; with an upright man thou wilt shew thyself upright; With the pure thou wilt shew thyself pure; and with the froward thou wilt shew thyself froward. For thou wilt save the afflicted people; but wilt bring down high looks. For thou wilt light my candle: the LORD my God will enlighten my darkness. For by thee I have run through a troop; and by my God have I leaped over a wall." Psalms 18:24-29.

Read Psalm 18 and write down what you can share of what He has given you:

_____

_____

_____

_____

_____

_____

_____

_____

_____

"Blessed be the LORD, because he hath heard the voice of my supplications. The LORD is my strength and my shield; my heart trusted in him, and I am helped: therefore my heart greatly rejoiceth; and with my song will I praise him. The LORD is their strength, and he is the saving strength of his anointed. Save thy people, and bless thine inheritance: feed them also, and lift them up for ever." Psalms 28:6-9.

Lasting Legacy

Treasure, shares, inheritance, and the list can go on about all that we value, but what about the legacy we leave behind? Our testimony should be treasured, because that is what we will be remembered by once we leave this earth. What legacy will you be known for? Often, we hear that someone has died, and their character, their "goodness" is emphasized. It's not just what we say, but what we do, how we live, how we treat others, what we do for Christ is the legacy we leave.

"There is treasure to be desired and oil in the dwelling of the wise; but a foolish man spendeth it up. He that followeth after righteousness and mercy findeth life, righteousness, and honour." Proverbs 21:20-21.

Will you pass into the realm of forgotten ones after a few years beyond your death? Or will you be remembered for wisely following after righteousness, searching for celestial treasures, and sharing the love of Christ with everyone around you? Will you have a legacy, and will it be a lasting one?

Remember these verses from earlier golden walks through Scripture?

"A good name is rather to be chosen than great riches, and loving favour rather than silver and gold. The rich and poor meet together: the LORD is the maker of them all." Proverbs 22:1-2.

"By humility and the fear of the LORD are riches, and honour, and life." Proverbs 22:4.

We have walked down the hall of faith in Hebrews 11, we have seen those faces who shine forth, like a radiant gem, their faith and trust in God. They had a testimony that has been repeated through the eons of time for our example and ensample. What are you leaving behind as a message to those coming after you? Will it just be an earthly inheritance, or like the virtuous woman touted in Proverbs 31, a lasting legacy for others to seek righteousness and godliness?

Are you searching to be rich in faith, hope, and love? Will you be known for sharing patience and lovingkindness, a good name that isn't about the wealth and fame of this world, but the spiritual wealth and faith of the world yet to come?

When you write your last will and testament, you are attesting to what you have to give, testifying that you are able to bestow it upon your beneficiaries. This is often the only legacy that people see, or care about. I urge you to leave a lasting spiritual legacy to your family, friends, and community.

Kicking Up Gold Dust

Surely, by now, as you have been mining, digging, and searching for the treasures in the Word of God, you should be covered in gold or diamond dust! Many treasures require time, work, and perseverance to collect, use, and share. However, you can't fail to walk down the golden road to Zion and not begin kicking up gold dust! We have walked through some of the Psalms and Proverbs, veritable gold mines that talk about gold and silver, precious stones, and things of value. The Bible is so full of treasure that you should be covered in it, bejeweled and bedecked with all manner of spiritual treasure.

Let's kick up some gold dust together!

Look up these references and write down what sparkling gems you find glittering within:

"The fining pot is for silver, and the furnace for gold: but the LORD trieth the hearts." Proverbs 17:3.

_____

"A gift is as a precious stone in the eyes of him that h it: whithersoever it turneth, it prospereth." Proverbs 17:8.

_____

"Better is little with the fear of the LORD than great treasure and trouble therewith." Proverbs 15:16.

_____

"A good man leaveth an inheritance to his children's children: and the wealth of the sinner is laid up for the just." Proverbs 13:22.

_____

"The words of the LORD are pure words: as silver tried in a furnace of earth, purified seven times. Thou shalt keep them, O LORD, thou shalt preserve them from this generation for ever." Psalms 12:6-7.

_____

"The LORD is the portion of mine inheritance and of my cup: thou maintainest my lot. The lines are fallen unto me in pleasant places; yea, I have a goodly heritage. I will bless the LORD, who hath given me counsel: my reins also instruct me in the night seasons. I have set the LORD always before me: because he is at my right hand, I shall not be moved. Therefore my heart is glad, and my glory rejoiceth: my flesh also shall rest in hope. For thou wilt not leave my soul in hell; neither wilt thou suffer thine Holy One to see corruption. Thou wilt shew me the path of life: in thy presence is fulness of joy; at thy right hand there are pleasures for evermore." Psalms 16:5-11.

The Royal Symphony

While kicking up gold dust with you, I found myself hearing the silver tones of the Psalms and other Scriptures ringing their praises to the King of kings. Praise is good and comely, so let's dive into the depths of praise to our King!

"For this cause I bow my knees unto the Father of our Lord Jesus Christ, Of whom the whole family in heaven and earth is named, That he would grant you, according to the riches of his glory, to be strengthened with might by his Spirit in the inner man; That Christ may dwell in your hearts by faith; that ye, being rooted and grounded in love, May be able to comprehend with all saints what is the breadth, and length, and depth, and height; And to know the love of Christ, which passeth knowledge, that ye might be filled with all the fulness of God. Now unto him that is able to do exceeding abundantly above all that we ask or think, according to the power that worketh in us, Unto him be glory in the church by Christ Jesus throughout all ages, world without end. Amen." Ephesians 3:14-21.

Now, in this position of worship, read Psalm 145 and, like the writers of old, extol the name of the Lord and all the wondrous things He has done for you!

Praise ye the LORD.
Praise God in his sanctuary:
Praise him in the firmament of his power.
Praise him for his mighty acts:
Praise him according to his excellent greatness.
Praise him with the sound of the trumpet:
Praise him with the psaltery and harp.
Praise him with the timbrel and dance:
Praise him with stringed instruments and organs.
Praise him upon the loud cymbals:

Praise him upon the high sounding cymbals.
Let every thing that hath breath praise the LORD.
Praise ye the LORD. Psalms 150.

Treasured Trials

What an odd title to think about, but let's ponder this concept. Are there trials that you have endured and made it through that made your faith stronger, your courage more obvious, your closeness to the Lord more pronounced? We often fall into the trap of thinking that we should not have to endure anything. We have touched on various things to treasure, but we do not want to consider trials to be a treasure to search for as something precious.

Immediately my mind reiterates this passage in the book of James. *"My brethren, count it all joy when ye fall into divers temptations; Knowing this, that the trying of your faith worketh patience. But let patience have her perfect work, that ye may be perfect and entire, wanting nothing. If any of you lack wisdom, let him ask of God, that giveth to all men liberally, and upbraideth not; and it shall be given him."* James 1:2-6. The treasure we see here is patience and joy!

Another passage states, *"Thou therefore endure hardness, as a good soldier of Jesus Christ. No man that warreth entangleth himself with the affairs of this life; that he may please him who hath chosen him to be a soldier. And if a man also strive for masteries, yet is he not crowned, except he strive lawfully."* 2 Timothy 2:3-5. This shows us that our treasure only comes when we are experienced, seasoned soldiers who endure the fight until the end.

We read treasured passages of saints of faith in the Scriptures who suffered what seems like unimaginable things, and they persevered with patient faith as God orchestrated their trials to make them stronger and brighter vessels to place His treasure within. While we have often claimed such heroes of the faith as our favorite and treasure their stories, we do not like to think that such things might or should happen to us as God's saints of faith.

While listening to a preacher from years gone by on the radio this week, he was speaking of that great saint named Job. Even the unsaved have heard of Job, there is so much we can learn from his life and his walk with God. However, the preacher went on to defend Job's wife! Think about this for a moment and treasure it, as her trial that also worked patience. God did not kill her, but He did strip her of everything as well. Yet, in the end, she was doubly blessed, just like Job, her patient husband. She lost ten children, ten is the number of testing here, but she was replenished with ten more, the number of testimony. Can you begin to imagine how her life was AFTER this horrific short time of trials upon trials? Their trials have become our treasured bastion of patience.

Maybe you aren't called to walk into a fiery furnace or face literal giants on the battlefield, maybe you won't lose all your children and possessions, or maybe you won't have to sit in a den filled with hungry lions, yet, you may have to endure hardness custom designed just for you! Will you prepare yourself for this act of faith now? When this time of trial is over, will it make you stronger and increase your faith? It can and will if you choose to let this trial bring you closer to your true Treasure, the Creator of all things!

"Go to now, ye rich men, weep and howl for your miseries that shall come upon you. Your riches are corrupted, and your garments are motheaten. Your gold and silver is cankered; and the rust of them shall be a witness against you, and shall eat your flesh as it were fire. Ye have heaped treasure together for the last days. Behold, the hire of the labourers who have reaped down your fields, which is of you kept back by fraud, crieth: and the cries of them which have reaped are entered into the ears of the Lord of sabaoth. Ye have lived in

pleasure on the earth, and been wanton; ye have nourished your hearts, as in a day of slaughter." James 5:1-5.

Sadly, we would rather think of treasure as stated above, to our own detriment and spiritual demise.

"Be patient therefore, brethren, unto the coming of the Lord. Behold, the husbandman waiteth for the precious fruit of the earth, and hath long patience for it, until he receive the early and latter rain. Be ye also patient; stablish your hearts: for the coming of the Lord draweth nigh." James 5:7-8. Our Lord is waiting for the trying of our faith to produce spiritual fruit, He is coming to gather His harvest.

"Beloved, think it not strange concerning the fiery trial which is to try you, as though some strange thing happened unto you: But rejoice, inasmuch as ye are partakers of Christ's sufferings; that, when his glory shall be revealed, ye may be glad also with exceeding joy. If ye be reproached for the name of Christ, happy are ye; for the spirit of glory and of God resteth upon you: on their part he is evil spoken of, but on your part he is glorified. But let none of you suffer as a murderer, or as a thief, or as an evildoer, or as a busybody in other men's matters. Yet if any man suffer as a Christian, let him not be ashamed; but let him glorify God on this behalf." 1 Peter 4:12-16.

What trials in your life can now be viewed as treasured?

Clothed With Majesty

"Honour and majesty are before him: strength and beauty are in his sanctuary. Give unto the LORD, O ye kindreds of the people, give unto the LORD glory and strength. Give unto the LORD the glory due unto his name: bring an offering, and come into his courts. O worship the LORD in the beauty of holiness: fear before him, all the earth." Psalms 96:6-9.

"As for the beauty of his ornament, he set it in majesty..." Ezekiel 7:20.

"The LORD reigneth, he is clothed with majesty; the LORD is clothed with strength, wherewith he hath girded himself..." Psalms 93:1.

Our King of kings is so majestic, even His appearance is hard to describe, although John, in Revelation, did what he could to help us envision it from a human perspective. We know that the saints will wear unspotted, linen robes of white in the Celestial City, but what are we wearing now?

We are clothed in human flesh, you may say, but as the saved by grace, blood-washed Bride of Christ, we too have been robed in heavenly garments this side of eternity. Let me describe this for you! The love of God that is shown through us is like golden threads woven throughout our living tapestry. His forgiveness of our sins is a much-desired daily robe of righteousness, but the added blessings that He so freely bestows upon us are like strands of diamonds.

Many people have, for years, followed the fashion trends of the earthly royal families, designing clothes to match their royal robes. Should we not even the more desire to be garbed in Heaven's finest whilst here upon earth? While scrolling through what sort of designs and fashions the current royal families wear in hopes to give you a picture in your mind to fasten upon, I came across a royal designer named Beulah!

Stunned to find such a Scriptural name for a royal designer, the correlation was not lost in application. Beulah is a Hebrew word for Bride or one who is married. Grab this treasure, dear one, don't let it be lost to you! We are the Bride of Christ, and in Isaiah we hear this is the name given to the land of Israel, the chosen people of God. He is clothed in majesty, but we are clothed in the raiment and finery of His bride, bedecked with jewels and treasures untold. Can you picture yourself thusly?

"For Zion's sake will I not hold my peace, and for Jerusalem's sake I will not rest, until the righteousness thereof go forth as brightness, and the salvation thereof as a lamp that burneth. And the Gentiles shall see thy righteousness, and all kings thy glory: and thou shalt be called by a new name, which the mouth of the LORD shall name. Thou shalt also be a crown of glory in the hand of the LORD, and a royal diadem in the hand of thy God. Thou shalt no more be termed Forsaken; neither shall thy land any more be termed Desolate: but thou shalt be called Hephzibah, and thy land Beulah: for the LORD delighteth in thee, and thy land shall be married." Isaiah 62:1-4.

If the earthly royal families are wise enough to choose a designer named Beulah, how much more should we desire to be robed in the treasured garments from the very Creator who is beautifully clothed with majesty?

The next time someone asks you where you got your clothes and shining beauty from, tell them you got yours from the Master Designer of all, Who is making ready our linen robes for Beulah Land.

What Are You Looking For?

Our study continues on searching and finding treasure in a spiritual aspect. What are you looking for? There are thrill seekers, talent searches, true love seekers, fame seekers and followers, and the list goes on. Everyone is always in search of something or someone. It's not necessarily that we have lost it, we just haven't found what we are looking for to satisfy our need or desire.

Deep down inside, we are all seeking Jesus, and yet we often don't realize we even have Him when He is right there waiting to be found!

"Judas then, having received a band of men and officers from the chief priests and Pharisees, cometh thither with lanterns and torches and weapons. Jesus therefore, knowing all things that should come upon him, went forth, and said unto them, Whom seek ye? They answered him, Jesus of Nazareth. Jesus saith unto them, I am he. And Judas also, which betrayed him, stood with them. As soon then as he had said unto them, I am he, they went backward, and fell to the ground. Then asked he them again, Whom seek ye? And they said, Jesus of Nazareth. Jesus answered, I have told you that I am he: if therefore ye seek me, let these go their way:" John 18:3-8. These sought Jesus to do Him harm, if you will, but they did not even realize He was the person they were actually looking for!

"But Mary stood without at the sepulchre weeping: and as she wept, she stooped down, and looked into the sepulchre, And seeth two angels in white sitting, the one at the head, and the other at the feet, where the body of Jesus had lain. And they say unto her, Woman, why weepest thou? She saith unto them, Because they have taken away my Lord, and I know not where they have laid him. And when she had thus said, she turned herself back, and saw Jesus standing, and knew not that it was

Jesus. Jesus saith unto her, Woman, why weepest thou? whom seekest thou? She, supposing him to be the gardener, saith unto him, Sir, if thou have borne him hence, tell me where thou hast laid him, and I will take him away. Jesus saith unto her, Mary. She turned herself, and saith unto him, Rabboni; which is to say, Master. Jesus saith unto her, Touch me not; for I am not yet ascended to my Father: but go to my brethren, and say unto them, I ascend unto my Father, and your Father; and to my God, and your God." John 20:11-17.

Here is someone who loved Jesus beyond description, yet her perception of circumstances blinded her to the truth of Who was standing in front of her, the very One she was seeking. Are you seeking Jesus? We have looked at the following verses before, let's review: *"But seek ye first the kingdom of God, and his righteousness; and all these things shall be added unto you."* Matthew 6:33-34.

When Jesus is Who you seek, then you are seeking true Treasure. As I was looking at the word "seeking," I noticed something very special about the location of the letters in this word. Do you see it yet?

Let's break the word into two words; what words do you see now?

SEE KING

Sometimes, the very word we use is the answer to our question!

When you see the King of kings, you have all that you'll ever need.

"But without faith it is impossible to please him: for he that cometh to God must believe that he is, and that he is a rewarder of them that diligently seek him." Hebrews 11:6.

Today, *See King* Jesus, and you'll never seek for another treasure or thrill.

Exalted Dust

What an odd phrase; what could exalted dust be? Is it possible to have exalted dust? In Proverbs 8, we hear from the voice of wisdom. Wisdom, in this chapter, instructs us to *"Receive my instruction, and not silver; and knowledge rather than choice gold. For wisdom is better than rubies; and all the things that may be desired are not to be compared to it."* Proverbs 8:10-11. This whole chapter bears reading, but you will need to desire to do that for yourself.

As you read what wisdom is instructing you, verse twenty-six is so easy to just skim through, for I have done this every time. A preacher drew my attention to it. Let's look at verse twenty-six together.

"While as yet he had not made the earth, nor the fields, nor the highest part of the dust of the world." Proverbs 8:26.

Wisdom was there before anything was created, yet look at that phrase "the highest part of the dust of the world." This preacher then referred to this verse: *"And the LORD God formed man of the dust of the ground, and breathed into his nostrils the breath of life; and man became a living soul."* Genesis 2:7.

God took some dust and elevated it, exalted it, if you would, by forming it into man. We seek gold dust, or diamond dust, and even just some grains of these can make one rich. God chose simple, dirty dust to create His most treasured creation, man.

We see that Abraham understood that he was but higher dust when he was speaking to God; *"And Abraham answered and said, Behold now, I have taken upon me to speak unto the Lord, which am but dust and ashes:"* Genesis 18:27.

However, there were evil men who did not understand where they came from or how God had exalted dust into humanity.

"Then the word of the LORD came to Jehu the son of Hanani against Baasha, saying, Forasmuch as I exalted thee out of the dust, and made thee prince over my people Israel; and thou hast walked in the way of Jeroboam, and hast made my people Israel to sin, to provoke me to anger with their sins;" 1 Kings 16:1-3.

Let us not be ignorant and foolish like the wicked kings of old. Let us remember what we are and run to our Creator with hearts of humility and obedience.

"Like as a father pitieth his children, so the LORD pitieth them that fear him. For he knoweth our frame; he remembereth that we are dust." Psalms 103:13-14.

Garden of Gems

There is so much reference to treasure throughout Scripture. Through our various treasure hunts, we have come across multiple references of wisdom and how it's compared to precious stones and its value is more than we can fathom. How do we get wisdom?

"It cannot be gotten for gold, neither shall silver be weighed for the price thereof. It cannot be valued with the gold of Ophir, with the precious onyx, or the sapphire. The gold and the crystal cannot equal it: and the exchange of it shall not be for jewels of fine gold. No mention shall be made of coral, or of pearls: for the price of wisdom is above rubies. The topaz of Ethiopia shall not equal it, neither shall it be valued with pure gold." Job 28:15-19.

In all simplicity, how do we get anything of value in our lives? It comes from God, given to us, to use for His glory. God wants to grow it in us. We are His garden of gems!

"Surely there is a vein for the silver, and a place for gold where they fine it. Iron is taken out of the earth, and brass is molten out of the stone. He setteth an end to darkness, and searcheth out all perfection: the stones of darkness, and the shadow of death." Job 28:1-3.

"The stones of it are the place of sapphires: and it hath dust of gold." Job 28:6.

The very first place God chose for man to live was in a garden. This garden was described in terms that sound like paradise to us. *"And the LORD God planted a garden eastward in Eden; and there he put the man whom he had formed. And out of the ground made the LORD God to grow every tree that is pleasant to the sight, and good for food; the tree of life also in the midst of the garden, and the tree of knowledge of good and evil. And a river went out of Eden to water the garden; and from thence it was parted, and became into four heads. The name of the first is Pison: that is it which compasseth the whole land of Havilah, where there is gold; And the gold of that land is good: there is bdellium and the onyx stone. And the name of the second river is Gihon: the same is it that compasseth the whole land of Ethiopia. And the name of the third river is Hiddekel: that is it which goeth toward the east of Assyria. And the fourth river is Euphrates. And the LORD God took the man, and put him into the garden of Eden to dress it and to keep it."* Genesis 2:8-15.

Sadly, man failed in this garden of Eden, but God still has a garden of gems in you and me as His children. *"I am the true vine, and my Father is the husbandman. Every branch in me that beareth not fruit he taketh away: and every branch that beareth fruit, he purgeth it, that it may bring forth more fruit. Now ye are clean through the word which I have spoken unto you. Abide in me, and I in you. As the branch cannot bear fruit of itself, except it abide in the vine; no more can ye, except ye abide in me. I am the vine, ye are the branches: He that abideth in me, and I in him, the same bringeth forth much fruit: for without me ye can do nothing. If a man abide not in me, he is cast forth as a branch, and is withered; and men gather them, and cast them into the fire, and they are burned. If ye abide in me, and my words abide in you, ye shall ask what ye will, and it shall be done unto you. Herein is my Father glorified, that ye bear much fruit; so shall ye be my disciples."* John 15:1-8.

With God-given wisdom, you can grow in God's beautiful garden of spiritual gems.

Garnets to Garner

We attribute ideals and symbolism to gemstones, even using gemstones to signify every month of the year in celebration of our birthdays. We call these birthstones. It has become so normalized that we no longer think it even remotely strange.

The very first month of the year is allotted to the garnet, a deep reddish-hued stone. When you research what the garnet symbolizes, you find a myriad of explanations, depending on which ideal or belief you lean towards. A recurring theme seems to be about protection, strength, or love.

Which ideals or beliefs do you collect to yourselves? We hold traditions as sacred that have been passed down through family heritage. In fact, sometimes what we treasure or collect, hence the word "garner," is more valuable to us than spiritual treasures.

A garnet is considered a semi-precious stone; it's value it not as significant as other stones that are deemed more precious. Why do we value lesser things over the more important things? Throughout this treasure hunt, we have attributed spiritual applications to treasure that is considered most precious. However, in our lives we tend to hang on to and search out things that glitter but aren't gold. We like bling and sparkly things, but they are all fake. The industry for fake gems is far more lucrative as most people cannot afford the real treasure.

If you look through all the birthstones to signify each month, you'll find that very few of them are more than semi-precious in value. When King Jesus makes up the jewels for His crown, they are those who are precious, blood-bought, redeemed souls. Their value was worth dying for! We are indeed precious in His sight.

Your true birthstone is the Chief Cornerstone, the Lord Jesus Christ. *"He that hath an ear, let him hear what the Spirit saith unto the churches; To him that overcometh will I give to eat of the hidden manna, and will give him a white stone, and in the stone a new name written, which no man knoweth saving he that receiveth it."* Revelation 2:17.

Doesn't this verse intrigue you? He will give the saints who overcome a white stone with a new name written on it. I would rather garner these types of spiritual stones than semi-precious family heirlooms, fake idealism, and paltry traditions.

Heavenly Hues

True saints of God are mesmerized by the stunning beauty that is described in Revelation of Heaven itself and the city of the New Jerusalem. We can pore over these verses and descriptions and never fully grasp such a sight that we will behold. Sit for a minute and think about all the wondrous hues that will be there. Green around the very throne of God, huge lustrous pearls, translucent gold, gemstones so fine that we would need to pick our jaw up off the floor if they were here on our current earth.

The many hues are so divinely designed that they do not clash or seem garish. *"By faith Abraham, when he was called to go out into a place which he should after receive for an inheritance, obeyed; and he went out, not knowing whither he went. By faith he sojourned in the land of promise, as in a strange country, dwelling in tabernacles with Isaac and Jacob, the heirs with him of the same promise: For he looked for a city which hath foundations, whose builder and maker is God."* Hebrews 11:8-10.

Abraham was certainly extremely wealthy, but his most sought-after treasure was not granted within his lifetime. Instead, by faith, he looked not just for the promised land for his offspring but for the New Jerusalem! When God designs and builds anything, its sheer beauty will contain every hue of the rainbow and probably more.

We get so caught up in our earthly travels, our bucket lists, places to see, and things to do, that we lose sight of why we are actually here. The treasure we are to collect is to have spiritual returns, not a paltry, earthly souvenir.

How many times after a storm do you look for that rainbow? When spring arrives, the new growth, the verdant vibrancy of green sprouts, and budding flowers all seem to fill us with the very air of expectancy. You can tell by the creation of the very planet that we live on that God LOVES color!

If you think our planet is beautiful now, just imagine what it will be when the sin curse is no longer upon the new earth and the New Jerusalem is seen descending down from the new Heaven. *"And I John saw the holy city, new Jerusalem, coming down from God out of heaven, prepared as a bride adorned for her husband."* Revelation 21:2.

"And he carried me away in the spirit to a great and high mountain, and shewed me that great city, the holy Jerusalem, descending out of heaven from God, Having the glory of God: and her light was like unto a stone most precious, even like a jasper stone, clear as crystal; And had a wall great and high, and had twelve gates, and at the gates twelve angels, and names written thereon, which are the names of the twelve tribes of the children of Israel: On the east three gates; on the north three gates; on the south three gates; and on the west three gates. And the wall of the city had twelve foundations, and in them the names of the twelve apostles of the Lamb. And he that talked with me had a golden reed to measure the city, and the gates thereof, and the wall thereof. And the city lieth foursquare, and the length is as large as the breadth: and he measured the city with the reed, twelve thousand furlongs. The length and the breadth and the height of it are equal. And he measured the wall thereof, an hundred and forty and four cubits, according to the measure of a man, that is, of the angel. And the building of the wall of it was of jasper: and the city was pure gold, like unto clear glass. And the foundations of the wall of the city were garnished with all manner of precious stones. The first foundation was jasper; the second, sapphire; the third, a chalcedony; the fourth, an emerald; The fifth, sardonyx; the sixth, sardius; the seventh, chrysolite; the eighth, beryl; the ninth, a topaz; the tenth, a chrysoprasus; the eleventh, a jacinth; the twelfth, an amethyst. And the twelve gates were twelve pearls; every several gate was

of one pearl: and the street of the city was pure gold, as it were transparent glass." Revelation 21:10-21.

Are you looking for that city of Heavenly hues?

For-Ged About It

Ever apologize to someone, and they say the now iconic reply, "For ged about it"? Now, you can add a lot more letters to this heavily accented response, but if you just break it down to a simple phonetic phrase, you come up with the above spelling. Now look closer, do you see the word "forged"? What does a forge do?

It uses a multi-layered process to heat and usually hammer things into a desired shaped object or tool. In fact, we use the phrase "hammer out our differences," alluding to this very process. Our relationships are often forged in the heat of trial and conflict.

The most valuable tool in this forging of friendships is forgiveness. It's the very cornerstone of our salvation and the necessary steel that makes us stronger in our faith and fellowship.

How do you forge forgiveness? *"Let all bitterness, and wrath, and anger, and clamour, and evil speaking, be put away from you, with all malice: And be ye kind one to another, tenderhearted, forgiving one another, even as God for Christ's sake hath forgiven you."* Ephesians 4:31-32.

Forging forgiveness is paramount; it is a treasure that we must daily seek and share. *"For if ye forgive men their trespasses, your heavenly Father will also forgive you: But if ye forgive not men their trespasses, neither will your Father forgive your trespasses."* Matthew 6:14-15.

Every book in the Bible has this steel cord running through it, binding, building, and blessing those who use this often rare treasure. *"Therefore if thou bring thy gift to the altar, and there rememberest that thy brother hath ought against thee; Leave there thy gift before the altar, and go thy way; first be reconciled to thy brother, and then come and offer thy gift."* Matthew 5:23-24.

May you grant forgiveness to any and all more than seventy times seven and "for ged about it." Just like God does with our sin.

"But this shall be the covenant that I will make with the house of Israel; After those days, saith the LORD, I will put my law in their inward parts, and write it in their hearts; and will be their God, and they shall be my people. And they shall teach no more every man his neighbour, and every man his brother, saying, Know the LORD: for they shall all know me, from the least of them unto the greatest of them, saith the LORD: for I will forgive their iniquity, and I will remember their sin no more." Jeremiah 31:33-34.

That's Top Shelf

Top shelf quality, the finest and best quality of a substance or product, is set aside in a special place, the top shelf. If we, as humans, treasure the quality of things and reserve special places for them that even denotes their quality, why would we not do this with our testimony, our walk with the Lord?

When I think about a treasure that we have here with us on earth that should be of the top-shelf category, sanctification comes to mind. *"Sanctify yourselves therefore, and be ye holy: for I am the LORD your God. And ye shall keep my statutes, and do them: I am the LORD which sanctify you."* Leviticus 20:7-8.

Throughout Scripture, this command is reiterated: to sanctify, to set apart. The book of Leviticus has numerous verses about how to sanctify things you have unto the Lord. We no longer live under the Mosaic Law, but we have it as an example. When was the last time you set apart something for the Lord? Did you give Him the best of what you have?

We already know God wants all of us; He redeemed us for Himself. However, He expects us to live holy, set-apart lives for His service. Is He getting top-shelf quality out of what you do for Him? When Jesus prayed for His disciples, He stated that they were sanctified. His truth sanctifies us.

"But sanctify the Lord God in your hearts: and be ready always to give an answer to every man that asketh you a reason of the hope that is in you with meekness and fear:" 1 Peter 3:15-16.

List some things that need to be set apart in your life, your home, your family.

_____

_____

God the Father gave His very best, His Son, Jesus Christ; only the best would do. Sadly, I think God gets our leftovers, or a miserly crumb, not top shelf material on a daily basis.

Miner Profits

While listening to a children's program on the radio, the question was asked, can you name the twelve minor prophets in the Bible? Oddly enough, I never realized that all those twelve books were in order at the end of the Old Testament. Neither did I recognize their value as a whole treasure-themed section of Scripture. When you hear the word "MINOR," you can mistake it for the word "MINER." Since we are to be miners of God's Word, let's see the value that we can profit from by looking at the twelve MINOR PROPHETS.

The rewards that we receive from studying these twelve books, although small in length, are rich in profitable lessons.

Hosea is about relationship, redemption, reconciliation, and restoration.

Joel is about returning to God, restoration, and repentance.

Amos urges repentance, a plea to not reject God and His men, with a reminder that religious acts are not enough to satisfy our redemption from sin.

Do you see a recurring theme? Let us continue to unearth more from these miners of God's riches.

As we continue, we see Obadiah speak about retributive justice and the righteous renewed.

Jonah is a message of God's redemption, but He had to redeem the rebellious messenger first. Repentance is a recurring theme in this book, with a reward of the promise of the resurrection as found elsewhere quoted by Jesus, Himself. *"Then certain of the scribes and of the Pharisees answered, saying, Master, we would see a sign from thee. But he answered and said unto them, An evil and adulterous generation seeketh after a sign; and there shall no sign be given to it, but the sign of the prophet Jonas: For as Jonas was three days and three nights in the whale's belly; so shall the Son of man be three days and three nights in the heart of the earth. The men of Nineveh shall rise in judgment with this generation, and shall condemn it: because they repented at the preaching of Jonas; and, behold, a greater than Jonas is here."* Matthew 12:38-41.

Our next Minor Miner is Micah. Again, he speaks about God's reward for those who repent and are restored with a renewal of the covenant. He admonishes those who rebel.

Nahum continues the theme of righteous judgment and retribution. Yes, all of the "R" words fit in each of these books!

As we come closer to the close of these mines in Scripture, we find Habakkuk, who requests us to rejoice in God, a reminder to rely on God and to always remember God. This book had other key "R" words. Take a moment to read the three chapters and underline all the words that start with "R".

"Although the fig tree shall not blossom, neither shall fruit be in the vines; the labour of the olive shall fail, and the fields shall yield no meat; the flock shall be cut off from the fold, and there shall be no herd in the stalls: Yet I will rejoice in the LORD, I will joy in the God of my salvation. The LORD God is my strength, and he will make my feet like hinds' feet, and he will make me to walk upon mine high places." Habakkuk 3:17-19.

What will we see in Zephaniah, but yet again, the recurring theme of restoration. Haggai speaks of rebuilding and a relationship, whilst Zechariah heralds the Lord's return, the restoration, the return of His remnant, and the rebuilding that will take place.

As we walk through the Mine of Malachi, we are noticing the reinforcement of faith in God, a reminder of our responsibilities, and of the restoration of our relationship.

Sadly, we profit very little from these mines of richness in God's Word because their size and category dull our vision of the vast riches that we can mine and profit from these Minor Prophets.

Jewels By the Dozen

When you study the significance of the number twelve in Scripture, it speaks of God's order of things. We just saw twelve minor prophets that spoke of hope and mercy as only found in a restorative relationship with God.

Let's search out twelve more jewels in Scripture and highlight their value. For example, there are twelve tribes of Israel chosen by God, and there are the twelve apostles of Christ. There are also twelve books in the Bible that begin with the letter J. This letter "J" should immediately make us think of Jesus, the Beginning and the End of our very existence and in Whom our faith is anchored.

Let's look at these twelve books in the Bible whose names begin with the letter "J." The first book in the Bible that starts with the letter "J" is Joshua. This name and the theme of this book are a type of Christ. Joshua is a book about God's faithfulness to His covenant. This was completed when Jesus, as the promised Messiah, came and fulfilled that promise. God always keeps His covenants and promises! What a jewel to treasure as we read Joshua. Joshua is fitting to be the first book in this portrayal of Jesus through Scripture, as He is the First (and the Last).

Our second book is Judges, a sad portrayal of people being unfaithful to God and having to be judged. We can see throughout Scripture that each time that Jesus comes, the unfaithful are judged.

The third book is Job, three is the number of the Trinity. Job is known for his patience through undeserved suffering. This, too, is a picture of the undeserved suffering that Jesus Christ endured for the sole reason that He did not want any to perish.

The fourth Jewel is the book of Jeremiah. The theme of this book is that God keeps His promises; He wants to restore us. It looks to a new covenant, a relationship, instead of a religion. Jesus is the fulfillment of this promise to restore us and establish a relationship with us.

The book of Joel is placed in Scripture as the fifth book. This is the number usually congruent with grace. The theme of Joel is that salvation only comes through turning to Jehovah. We know that this means that there is no salvation in any other Name, but the Name of Jesus Christ. For by grace are ye saved through faith is the verse that comes to mind.

The Old Testament only has one more "J" book in it. This is our sixth jewel; six is the number of man. It makes perfect sense that the book of Jonah would be this sixth book. Themed throughout this book are sin and forgiveness, compassion for the wicked, and God's mercy. Jonah is referred to in Matthew 12:40 as a sign of Jesus's death as victory over sin. Was Jonah chosen because God KNEW He would be disobedient? Would there have been a sign of Jonas if he had obeyed the first time? It was stated that maybe God chose to save Jonah in the belly of the great fish and not let him perish so that he could be used as a sign in Matthew 12:40. He chose Jonah to illustrate that God will save us out of our disobedience.

Our seventh jewel-encrusted book is the first "J" book in the New Testament. This precious treasure is the Gospel of John. Dare we state that the placing of this book as the first book in this division of Scripture and it also being the seventh book in our list is intentional? Jesus is the First, and also, as the number seven denotes, He is perfect and complete. This treasure is only collected by receiving the Gospel. The word Gospel means the good news of salvation, thus the theme of this book. That ye might believe that Jesus is the Christ, the Son of God, and that believing you might have life through His Name.

The number eight is often used for "new beginnings." The second J book in the New Testament is James, the eighth book in this list. As a new creature in Christ, we are to begin growing in wisdom, faith, and obedience. We are to grow into spiritual maturity. This book reminds me of the warning of Judges, the second J book in the Old Testament.

Our ninth book in this cluster of jewels from Scripture is the book of 1 John. The number nine is synonymous with the fruit of the Spirit, which makes sense to come after the book of James. The theme of this book is highlighting the first fruit of the Spirit which is LOVE. This treasure given to us by the Holy Spirit is the central theme of this book! We will manifest this fruit when we have true doctrine, obedient living, and fervent devotion. This book parallels Job, with its Light vs. Darkness, and these are both the third book for each testament in the Bible.

As we have collected nine of the twelve jewels in our walk through the Bible, we must continue onward to the tenth book that starts with the letter "J" in Scripture. Ten is the number of Testimony, the book of 2 John instructs us to have a testimony of truth in love. Walk in the truth, and watch out for false doctrine. This book is a snapshot of the book of Jeremiah!

Third John, albeit a small book in size, is chock full of gems. It builds upon the previous two epistles of John in its message of love and truth and supporting others who walk in love and truth. We are to be steadfast in our doctrine and our fellowship and adhere to Biblical principles and standards for this fellowship. Don't skip the treasure that is to be found in this eleventh book that starts with "J."

The final book in our Bible that starts with J is Jude. God's judgment on rebellion is a parallel theme to Jonah! Be faithful, be obedient, be true!

We have a dozen Jewels in these "J" books in Scripture that brilliantly display God's foundation of faith and redemption. What wonder to fathom that these precious jewels were placed in such specific order and fashion.

Richer Than Croesus

History and tradition speak of King Midas, who lost his own daughter to his greed, or Croesus, who was vastly wealthy supposedly because of King Midas. We use the phrase "the Midas Touch" or "Rich as Croesus" even in our vernacular in modern times.

Too many people fall prey to the need for greed, filthy lucre, the love of money in their concept of success. What could possibly make you and me even richer than King Croesus?

How did you answer that question? In this quest for spiritual riches, by now you should have multiple answers. *"For as many as are led by the Spirit of God, they are the **sons of God**. For ye have not received the spirit of bondage again to fear; but ye have received the **Spirit of adoption,** whereby we cry, Abba, Father. The Spirit itself beareth witness with our spirit, that we are the* <u>children of God: And if children, then heirs;</u> ***heirs of*** ***God, and joint-heirs with Christ***; *if so be that we suffer with him, that we may be also glorified together."* Romans 8:14-17. Notice the phrases that, for the sake of this study, were highlighted and underlined for emphasis.

*"Beloved, now are we the **sons of God**, and it doth not yet appear what we shall be: but we know that, when he shall appear, we shall be like him; for we shall see him as he is. And every man that hath this hope in him purifieth himself, even as he is pure."* 1 John 3:2-3.

My finite mind cannot begin to comprehend this, but by faith, I know that you and I, once redeemed by His blood, are adopted by the Creator King, we are joint heirs, and this makes us richer than Croesus ever could imagine becoming. *"Who shall separate us from the love of Christ? shall tribulation, or distress, or persecution, or famine, or nakedness, or peril, or sword? As it is written, For thy sake we are killed all the day long; we are accounted as sheep for the slaughter. Nay, in all these things we are more than conquerors through him that loved us. For I am persuaded, that neither death, nor life, nor angels, nor principalities, nor powers, nor things present, nor things to come, Nor height, nor depth, nor any other creature, shall be able to separate us from the love of God, which is in Christ Jesus our Lord."* Romans 8:35-39.

That, my friend, is the best source of wealth we could ever want or dream up!

Lost Its Luster?!

There have been so many aspects of treasure that we have discovered, unearthed, and put on display for you to collect for your own treasure troves in your heart. However, the longer this study continues, there seems to be a treasure that we have really overlooked, and sadly in this day and age, it's no longer valued. In fact, in many of our churches, it has lost its luster and has become tarnished. What treasure do you think this might be?

By far, our marriages have become tarnished, devalued, and almost obsolete. If you are married, do you treasure and value your spouse? We have touched upon the thought that we, as the church, are the Bride of Christ. However, our own marriages are to be reflections of this! The very first thing that God did with His human creations was to make them man and wife! He officiated the first wedding ever!

"And the LORD God said, It is not good that the man should be alone; I will make him an help meet for him. And out of the ground the LORD God formed every beast of the field, and every fowl of the air; and brought them unto Adam to see what he would call them: and whatsoever Adam called every living creature, that was the name thereof. And Adam gave names to all cattle, and to the fowl of the air, and to every beast of the field; but for Adam there was not found an help meet for him." Genesis 2:18-20. Sorry guys, even a dog was not enough for what Adam needed.

"And the LORD God caused a deep sleep to fall upon Adam, and he slept: and he took one of his ribs, and closed up the flesh instead thereof; And the rib, which the LORD God had taken from man, made he a woman, and brought her unto the man. And Adam said, This is now bone of my bones, and flesh of my flesh: she shall be called Woman, because she was taken out of Man. Therefore shall a man leave his father and his mother,

and shall cleave unto his wife: and they shall be one flesh." Genesis 2:21-24.

Now, skip to where Jesus performs His first mentioned miracle; it was at a wedding! Paul, in his epistles with the Divine Writer telling him what to say, spells it all out so clearly. Satan has attacked this divine institution from its very inception in the garden!

For those of you who are married, think of your spouse. Do you treasure and value that person as the picture of Christ and His church? Has your relationship become tarnished and lost its luster?

Pull out the polish and spiritual cleanser of Ephesians 5:22-23, and let's reinstate the valued treasure of our marriages.

Quantifying Quality

Dear Reader, how often do we mistake quantity as the definition of wealth or riches? We often hear the phrase, "less is more," but we fall into the trap of always wanting more.

This devotional section could be on contentment, or envy, or jealousy and that all would apply. However, let's look at how little is much when God is in it, instead.

Faith is one of the treasures of the heart; repeatedly in Scripture, we are told that even the smallest measure of faith is a quantitative quality in God's eyes! *"And Jesus said unto them, Because of your unbelief: for verily I say unto you, If ye have faith as a grain of mustard seed, ye shall say unto this mountain, Remove hence to yonder place; and it shall remove; and nothing shall be impossible unto you."* Matthew 17:20.

"And the apostles said unto the Lord, Increase our faith. And the Lord said, If ye had faith as a grain of mustard seed, ye might say unto this sycamine tree, Be thou plucked up by the root, and be thou planted in the sea; and it should obey you." Luke 17:5-6.

Are you searching out great faith and ways to live it out in your life? Hint: It's usually attached to trials and affliction, neither of which we welcome, even to grow our faith!

Let's look at another quality that we all yearn for in the midst of trials and afflictions. Peace! We tend to think of peace as a quantity, instead of understanding that even a little peace, if from God, is HUGE!

"These things I have spoken unto you, that in me ye might have peace. In the world ye shall have tribulation: but be of good cheer; I have overcome the world." John 16:33.

"But the meek shall inherit the earth; and shall delight themselves in the abundance of peace." Psalms 37:11.

"Mark the perfect man, and behold the upright: for the end of that man is peace." Psalms 37:37.

"Great peace have they which love thy law: and nothing shall offend them." Psalms 119:165.

These verses about peace have qualifications to that peace, let's look at one more verse about peace. *"Peace I leave with you, my peace I give unto you: not as the world giveth, give I unto you. Let not your heart be troubled, neither let it be afraid."* John 14:27.

When your peace and your faith is in the Lord Jesus Christ, you have enough!

Little is truly much, when God is in it!

Jewel of Denial

In most instances, we think of denial as less than something to treasure. For this particular treasure hunt, I want us to focus on the jewel of denial.

"Then said Jesus unto his disciples, If any man will come after me, let him deny himself, and take up his cross, and follow me. For whosoever will save his life shall lose it: and whosoever will lose his life for my sake shall find it. For what is a man profited, if he shall gain the whole world, and lose his own soul? or what shall a man give in exchange for his soul? For the Son of man shall come in the glory of his Father with his angels; and then he shall reward every man according to his works." Matthew 16:24-27.

The jewel here is self-denial and seeking only spiritual treasure instead of self-righteousness and temporary pleasure. *"It is a faithful saying: For if we be dead with him, we shall also live with him: If we suffer, we shall also reign with him: if we deny him, he also will deny us: If we believe not, yet he abideth faithful: he cannot deny himself."* 2 Timothy 2:11-13.

Our reward for denying our sinful ways is to live and reign with Jesus! How do we use this jewel of denial? *"Know ye not that they which run in a race run all, but one receiveth the prize? So run, that ye may obtain. And every man that striveth for the mastery is temperate in all things. Now they do it to obtain a corruptible crown; but we an incorruptible. I therefore so run, not as uncertainly; so fight I, not as one that beateth the air: But I keep under my body, and bring it into subjection: lest that by any means, when I have preached to others, I myself should be a castaway."* 1 Corinthians 9:24-27.

The treasure here is the gift of temperance from the Holy Spirit, this fruit of self-control. We are in a race to obtain an eternal prize; we must, like any fighter or runner or athlete, keep our bodies in shape. This, of course, needs to start with our mindset. Self-denial starts with the training and control of our minds.

See Romans 12:1-2. What does it say our minds should be? _____

"For though we walk in the flesh, we do not war after the flesh: (For the weapons of our warfare are not carnal, but mighty through God to the pulling down of strong holds;) Casting down imaginations, and every high thing that exalteth itself against the knowledge of God, and bringing into captivity every thought to the obedience of Christ;" 2 Corinthians 10:3-5.

Self-control starts with the mind. This is where we can find the Jewel of Denial.

Do you have this particular treasure?

H.M.S. Bounty

His Majesty's Ship, or maybe we call it His Majesty's Service, either way, we are on board this ship of Zion. How did we get assigned to His service?

We had a bounty on our hearts. *"For when ye were the servants of sin, ye were free from righteousness. What fruit had ye then in those things whereof ye are now ashamed? for the end of those things is death. But now being made free from sin, and become servants to God, ye have your fruit unto holiness, and the end everlasting life. For the wages of sin is death; but the gift of God is eternal life through Jesus Christ our Lord."* Romans 6:20-23.

"For ye are bought with a price: therefore glorify God in your body, and in your spirit, which are God's." 1 Corinthians 6:20.

Jesus paid the price, the bounty we had on us, and now we serve Him. However, because the cost was so great, we owe Him our very lives. These same lives that were created to serve Him, He has promised to bountifully supply our needs.

English words are so wonderful in their kaleidoscope of definitions and usage. Many dictionaries agree that the word bounty has at least five different definitions, and each of these fit with our spiritual search for practical applications of these.

Bounty is summarily defined as liberality in giving, generosity, an abundance of something. It's also a reward or payment often given by a governing authority for acts that are beneficial to the state or for enlisting in the military.

Does James 1:5 come to mind?

The Psalms often repeat the phrase that the Lord has dealt bountifully. In 2 Corinthians, Paul speaks about giving, bountifully, abounding, and liberality. Let's head to the gangway and walk through these verses together.

"But this I say, He which soweth sparingly shall reap also sparingly; and he which soweth bountifully shall reap also bountifully. Every man according as he purposeth in his heart, so let him give; not grudgingly, or of necessity: for God loveth a cheerful giver. And God is able to make all grace abound toward you; that ye, always having all sufficiency in all things, may abound to every good work: (As it is written, He hath dispersed abroad; he hath given to the poor: his righteousness remaineth for ever. Now he that ministereth seed to the sower both minister bread for your food, and multiply your seed sown, and increase the fruits of your righteousness;) Being enriched in every thing to all bountifulness, which causeth through us thanksgiving to God. For the administration of this service not only supplieth the want of the saints, but is abundant also by many thanksgivings unto God; Whiles by the experiment of this ministration they glorify God for your professed subjection unto the gospel of Christ, and for your liberal distribution unto them, and unto all men; And by their prayer for you, which long after you for the exceeding grace of God in you. Thanks be unto God for his unspeakable gift." 2 Corinthians 9:6-15.

There is so much to study in this passage, will you take the time to reap the bounty that can be found as you sail along with His Majesty, Jesus Christ?

Koiné and the Barbarian

"I am debtor both to the Greeks, and to the Barbarians; both to the wise, and to the unwise. So, as much as in me is, I am ready to preach the gospel to you that are at Rome also." Romans 1:14-15.

We understand that Jesus paid our sin debt at Calvary, but when Paul here says he is a debtor to the Greeks and the Barbarians, he is not talking about money. Paul is, in fact, saying that he is obligated, nay, even commanded to share Christ with everyone regardless of their culture, background, or social standing.

Koiné is the Greek word for the language that was spoken during this time. In fact, our New Testament was largely written in this classic Greek. Paul was called by God to share the gift of the Gospel to both the educated Greek and other people groups classified as Barbarians. My Friends, unless you are Jew or Greek, then you are a Barbarian! Aren't you so glad that the ground is level at the cross?

This common salvation (Jude 1:3) is to be given to the upper class AND the commoners. What a debt that Paul felt he owed to all people groups to share Christ. His calling by God was his greatest treasure. Do you value obedience to God's call on your life as much as God treasures your faithfulness?

"Go ye therefore, and teach all nations, baptizing them in the name of the Father, and of the Son, and of the Holy Ghost: Teaching them to observe all things whatsoever I have commanded you: and, lo, I am with you alway, even unto the end of the world. Amen." Matthew 28:19-20.

"For there is no difference between the Jew and the Greek: for the same Lord over all is <u>rich</u> unto all that call upon him. For whosoever shall call upon the name of the Lord shall be saved." Romans 10:12-13.

What has God called you to do? He has called you to share the precious treasure of His Gospel to others regardless of who they are. You are in debt to Him; you owe your life to Him! Do you see yourself obligated to others to teach them about so great a salvation?

I am so thankful that Paul felt this great debt both to the Greeks and to the Barbarians, that the Koiné was a language that we still reference as Barbarians to understand this great treasure of the Gospel.

Lost Treasure

As we near the end of this journey of discovery, we have focused mainly on finding treasure that we can use here in our Christian lives, along with the treasure we store up in Heaven.

This idea of finding treasure has the obvious subconscious concept that it's lost or hidden! Whilst thinking about the idea of lost treasure, there came that sad realization that sometimes we collect treasure only to misplace it or lose it!

What sort of spiritual treasures do we tend to lose?

Hope? *"Hope deferred maketh the heart sick: but when the desire cometh, it is a tree of life."* Proverbs 13:12.

What might cause us to lose hope? *"And they said, There is no hope: but we will walk after our own devices, and we will every one do the imagination of his evil heart."* Jeremiah 18:12.

When we turn from the God of hope, we will lose His treasure of Hope! *"And thou hast removed my soul far off from peace: I forgat prosperity. And I said, My strength and my hope is perished from the LORD:"* Lamentations 3:17-18.

What else do we often lose that we once treasured? The above verse says we lose strength and peace as well! Too often, we let the storms of life rob us of our hope: *"Which when they had taken up, they used helps, undergirding the ship; and, fearing lest they should fall into the quicksands, strake sail, and so were driven. And we being exceedingly tossed with a tempest, the next day they lightened the ship; And the third day we cast out with our own hands the tackling of the ship. And when neither sun nor stars in many days appeared, and no small tempest lay on us, all hope that we should be saved was then taken away."* Acts 27:17-21.

When we turn from the Lord, abandon hope, and lose strength, we also lose the treasure of love: *"Nevertheless I have somewhat against thee, because thou hast left thy first love.*

Remember therefore from whence thou art fallen, and repent, and do the first works; or else I will come unto thee quickly, and will remove thy candlestick out of his place, except thou repent." Revelation 2:4-5.

This isn't just losing hope or losing love; it's deliberately leaving it! We have such vast spiritual treasure, however, for self-justified reasons we just walk away from it!!

How tragic!

What are some of your spiritual treasures that you have lost or have left?

_____

_____

_____

Last Treasure

Friends, what if today was your last day on earth? What would be the last thing that you would want to do? What about your last earthly thought as you take your last breath this side of Eternity? What would your last words be?

These thoughts often come to mind, yet, usually, we are not aware ahead of time when these very last things might be our last. We have many examples of the word "last" in our vocabulary usage. The Last Supper, the last call, the last person on earth, the last one out, all of these are commonly used, yet we don't think of our last treasure. Whatever the last thing you would want to be thinking or doing, is where your treasure and heart are. There is such a sense of finality to that word "last." Yet, for the believer, it's really the beginning of our eternity on the Other Side.

Only what is done for Christ will "LAST." There are many definitions of this word, but if this is the last entry of this devotional, what would you want it to help you discover? What final treasure do you need to collect? If our first treasure is salvation, and our souls are God's treasure, what would our last treasure be here on earth?

"And, behold, I come quickly; and my reward is with me, to give every man according as his work shall be. I am Alpha and Omega, the beginning and the end, the first and the last." Revelation 22:12-13.

"No man can come to me, except the Father which hath sent me draw him: and I will raise him up at the last day." John 6:44-45.

"But every man in his own order: Christ the firstfruits; afterward they that are Christ's at his coming. Then cometh the end, when he shall have delivered up the kingdom to God, even the Father; when he shall have put down all rule and all

authority and power. For he must reign, till he hath put all enemies under his feet. The last enemy that shall be destroyed is death." 1 Corinthians 15:23-26.

Reading all these Scriptures, with the emphasis on "last," there is so much comfort to know that because souls and service are treasured by God, the believer will be Home, safe at last!

Author's Note:

Thank you for going on this treasure hunt through Scripture with me. Although some of the references were re-used and some of the treasure was referenced repeatedly in various ways, my hope is that you eagerly collected it all into your spiritual treasure chest.

This devotional study was originally planned as a companion guide of Scripture to go with Book 2 in the Lady Jane Chronicles: Library of Treasure. My own personal study had garnered extra Scripture that I wanted to share. My wonderful editor told me that more than what I had originally collected was actually needed, thus the treasure hunt commenced!

This devotional study is able to be read and treasured without even reading the novels, however, I do hope you will want to read the source of the material that this devotional study was based upon.

Thank you to my amazing editor for entrusting this project to me, and to His Majesty, Jesus Christ, for sharing His wealth of Scripture with us.

www.ingramcontent.com/pod-product-compliance
Lightning Source LLC
LaVergne TN
LVHW051230080426
835513LV00016B/1499